Chaucer's Church

About the volume:

The purpose of *Chaucer's Church* is to provide clear, concise and reliable explanations of every term Chaucer uses that has a religious, liturgical, or ecclesiastical meaning. It uses a dictionary format, arranged according to Chaucer's spellings, to make information readily accessible for students, teachers, critics, and the general reader. The shorter entries present brief definitions which are more lively and illuminating than those in standard dictionaries or glossaries; the longer entries are in fact short essays, with suggestions for further reading, on broader or more complex topics. In all cases the entries concentrate on lucid and accurate presentation of the meanings that the terms had or could have had for Chaucer and a fourteenth-century audience.

The book is a compact but precise reference for readers of all levels of experience on the vocabulary of fourteenth-century religion, which is often unfamiliar or only hazily understood. A careful system of cross-references guides the reader to related terms, so that individual entries can be further explored in related or larger contexts. The book may also be browsed or read on its own, for the entries taken together, especially the brief essays, provide a coherent introduction to the Christian world of the late fourteenth century.

In *Chaucer's Church*, the editors have succeeded in compiling a volume that combines ease of use with readability and rigorous accuracy. This book provides convenient and trustworthy access to Chaucer's religious world.

About the authors:

Edward E. Foster received his A.B. from St Peter's College and his Ph.D. in English from the University of Rochester. He was a Fulbright Fellow at the University of Nottingham in 1986 and an Honorary Professor of English at the University of St Andrews in 1989–90. He has edited *King Arthur's Death: The Alliterative Morte Arthur and The Stanzaic Mort Arthure* and *Amiloun, Sir Amadace, and Robert of Cisyle* for Medieval Institute Publications. He has authored *Chaucer's Intellectual and Interpretative World: Nominalist Fiction* (Mellen Press) and has published studies of Chaucer and metrical romance in the *Chaucer Review* and other journals. For the last twenty years he has been Professor of English at Whitman College. He holds the Schwabacher Professorship of English at Whitman and an honorary D.H.L. from Albertson College.

David H. Carey took a B.A. from St John's College (at Annapolis, MD), S.T.B. and M.A. in theology from Pontificia Universitas Gregoriana, and M.A. and Ph.D. in philosophy from the University of Pittsburgh. He was an Assistant Professor of Philosophy at Whitman College from 1989 to 1994, at which time he was tenured and promoted to Associate Professor.

Chaucer's Church

A Dictionary of Religious Terms in Chaucer

EDWARD E. FOSTER
AND
DAVID H. CAREY

Routledge
Taylor & Francis Group
LONDON AND NEW YORK

First published 2002 by Ashgate Publishing

Reissued 2018 by Routledge
2 Park Square, Milton Park, Abingdon, Oxon OX14 4RN
711 Third Avenue, New York, NY 10017, USA

Routledge is an imprint of the Taylor & Francis Group, an informa business

A Library of Congress record exists under LC control number: 2001053580

ISBN 13: 978-1-138-72511-9 (hbk)
ISBN 13: 978-1-138-72506-5 (pbk)
ISBN 13: 978-1-315-19204-8 (ebk)

Contents

Preface

Religion permeated life in the fourteenth century in a way that may be hard for a modern person to imagine. A united, if squabbling, Christianity was present to Chaucer and his contemporaries as a fact of daily life. Religious feasts and observances, veneration of the saints, familiarity with the stories of Scripture, and a present consciousness of the four last things—death, judgment, heaven, and hell—were embedded in the experiences and habits of mind of England in the High Middle Ages. Therefore, to understand Chaucer it is necessary to be familiar with the religious, ecclesiastical, and liturgical vocabulary that emanated from his world. The intention of this book is to provide ready access not only to the meanings of the religious vocabulary that Chaucer and his hearers took for granted, but also to suggest something of the resonance that the words and ideas would have had for Chaucer and his contemporaries. Religious language has a significance and potency in a world of faith that it cannot have in a more secular and diverse society. To re-create some of that resonance, we have endeavored to provide definitions beyond the kind of shorthand found in editions and glossaries, yet short of the comprehensive treatment that scholarly exegesis would provide—a kind of middle ground that improves the reader's context for understanding without the detail appropriate for a religious historian.

We have used as our base the *Riverside Edition* of Chaucer (gen. ed. Larry D. Benson. Boston: Houghton Mifflin Co., 1987) and the corresponding concordance: *A Complete Concordance to the Works of Geoffrey Chaucer*, ed. Akio Oizumi (New York: Olms-Weidman, 1991-). On the assumption that this book will primarily be used by readers who come upon a word or name in Chaucer and want a clarification of its meaning or significance beyond what a glossary would provide, we have arranged the terms in alphabetical order. We have enumerated all of the Chaucerian spellings under the same entry, using parentheses to indicate optional letters. We have not included all grammatical forms of the words on the grounds that this would be needlessly repetitive. Thus, we list "purvea(u)nce" and "purveyaunce", but provide no separate entry for "purveye". Since our expectation is that the reader will be moving from Chaucer's text to our definitions, we have not included line-number references, which are, in any case, fully detailed in the Chaucer Concordance.

Consistent judgments had to be made about what to include and what to leave out: essentially, where to draw the boundaries of "religious terms". We have included all terms that have a specifically religious meaning and terms with secular meanings if they also have an important religious imposition or implication. Thus, "astrologye" is not a specifically religious term, but it had wide-reaching religious significance as a challenge to orthodox beliefs concerning free will and the order of God's creation.

We have also included entries on all of the saints and Biblical figures mentioned in Chaucer, even if they are used only in passing or in oaths, in the conviction that information about these figures helps to replicate the intellectual furniture of Chaucer's and his audience's consciousness. It may not be crucial to know who St. Frideswyde or Lamech was, but in the aggregate these names gain importance because Chaucer and his fellows did know. Certainly the large array of saints, even if some are obscure, suggests something worth knowing about the fourteenth century's sense of this world and the next. Likewise, through sermons and iconography, Scriptural stories were broadly known even if popular reading of the Scriptures was difficult if not discouraged. (All Scriptural references are to the Revised Standard Version rather than to the Latin Vulgate Chaucer would have known.)

Contrarily, we have omitted nonce-words used only once by the Parson, and immediately defined in his sermon, pertaining to the categories of the deadly sins and their remedies, such as "superbie", "contumacie", "invidie", and "gule". We have, however, included similar words, like "luxurie" and "accidie", if they identify a major category of "deadly sin" or if they are used a number of times. Chaucer's use of synonyms for the seven deadly sins posed a different problem: e.g., "lust" and "luxurie", "anger" and "ire", "envie" and "covetise". Since these are all important and common terms, we have provided brief definitions of each under its own spelling, but have also referred the reader, in every case, to our longer contextual treatment of "deedly synnes". Nonce-words which are not internally defined, such as those used by the Summoner and the Host, are included and defined.

The most basic choice we had to make was with regard to how long the definitions should be. Our conclusion was that different words simply require different treatment. Our intention, overall, is to be informative but not comprehensive. Thus, most definitions are of moderate length—long enough to be helpful (we hope), but short enough to be efficient. There are, however, six terms for which we have intentionally provided unusually lengthy definitions because they provide such a rich context of Medieval religious thought and practice: Astrologye, Court Cristien (Ecclesiastical Court), C(h)rist, Marie (Seinte), Purveaunce, and Scripture. These definitions, taken together with nine others of more moderate length (Frere/friar, Heresye, Messe/Mass, Monk, Pardo(u)n, Pilgrimage, Pope, Predestinacioun, and Sacrement), although they do not constitute a systematic history, provide a broad overview of Chaucer's religious milieu as it manifests itself in his literary works, while preserving the format of the rest of this "dictionary". We have highlighted these fifteen entries by putting their headings in all capital letters for ease of identification. Reading these fifteen entries as a block may be compared to viewing the façade and rose window of a Gothic cathedral. These central images of stone and glass convey an ordered universe, a cosmos, in which the individual details found in the other parts of the cathedral can be contextualized. So, too, we hope to convey something of Chaucer's religious worldview in these more lengthy entries as an important context for making sense of the shorter entries. Also, in the longer entries, we have provided a concise definition early on, and then expanded insofar as we thought fuller treatment would illustrate the whole of fourteenth-century religious culture, and we have provided some suggestions for "Further Reading".

Naturally it was tempting to expand the number of such entries to include many more important words such as doctrine, deedly synnes, Purgatorie, and others, but we believe our selection represents the best compromise of inclusiveness and restraint in giving some terms special attention. At the other end of the spectrum we have included a few one-word definitions, but only when the Medieval spelling might obscure the connection to the obvious modern equivalent.

To make the definitions informative without devolving into undue repetition, we have used an internal system of cross-referencing so that the reader can see the significance of terms in the context of related terms if he or she so chooses. These cross-references are indicated by bold italics. In some cases the modern spelling is so different that we have included, in parentheses, the Medieval spelling to make the referenced entry clear, though we have not bothered with such obvious pairs, say, as absolution/absolucion or salvation/salvacion. In addition, the use of the word "indulgence" in a definition may be followed by a parenthetical "pardoun", the Medieval term for "indulgence" if checking that usage might be useful. Such cross-referencing is also used to refer the reader to longer treatments of related ideas such as "deedly synnes" for "pride" or "Court Cristien" (ecclesiastical courts) for "sumnour". If a useful cross-reference did not fit easily within the entry, it has been put at the end of the entry. As with the length of definitions, cross-referencing has been guided by our intention to make this book informative and friendly rather than ostentatious.

Nevertheless, the book may still be of some interest to those who would like to peruse it as a general orientation to Chaucer's religious vocabulary, or to those who are simply curious. For such readers, in addition to the longer entries mentioned above, we have provided an appendix that lists selected modern religious terms which are relevant to Chaucer but do not appear in Chaucer's language; for each we have indicated the Middle English entries under which information on these terms may be found. For example, the Incarnation of Christ is very important to fourteenth century religion; since Chaucer does not use the word, we have, in the appendix, directed the reader to the entry on "Christ", where the topic is addressed. Similarly, the doctrine of indulgences was a lively topic of controversy in Chaucer's time, but the word used was "pardoun". Thus, the appendix should help locate where some familiar and relevant terms are embedded in Chaucerian language.

Finally, just as this work is not a comprehensive religious history, neither is it, strictly speaking, literary criticism. No attempt has been made to use the definitions to argue any particular interpretation of Chaucer. We have, however, tried to limit definitions to senses which Chaucer could or did have in mind. Within definitions we have sometimes cited Chaucerian instances, but only insofar as such references clarify the meaning of the word or its context; our intention has not been to provide a critical reading of Chaucer.

We hope the result is a useful guide that extends far enough beyond dictionary definitions or textual annotations to create some sense of the resonance of Chaucer's religious vocabulary and sensibility.

Edward E. Foster, *Whitman College*
David Carey, *Whitman College*

Acknowledgements

We would like to thank Whitman College for its generous support particularly in the provision of sabbatical leaves for both authors. We would especially like to thank Hope Donovan for her invaluable editorial support including checking and correcting Scriptural references, formatting, and assistance in preparation of the manuscript.

Entries

abbay, abbey(e). A monastery, ordinarily housing not fewer than twelve religious of either sex. An abbey was different from a priory, which was the name for the residence of an autonomous religious foundation (one not connected with other "houses" under the same ***rule***) and presided over by a ***prior*** or ***prioress***. (See ***monk***.)

abbesse. The female superior in a religious community of twelve or more nuns (***nonne***). Originally the title applied to Benedictine foundations, but it was extended to the Second Order of St. Francis (Poor Clares) and gradually to communities living under other rules. Although an abbess had no spiritual jurisdiction and she could not perform priestly functions, she was the supreme domestic authority within her monastery. Abbesses were elected by the nuns of the community, but ordinarily they were women from privileged backgrounds, from powerful or distinguished families, and were likely, therefore, despite their cloistered vocation, to be present at important national and religious events from coronations to synods. (See ***monk***.)

abbot. The chief officer of a monastery, especially Benedictine. The abbot, like the other monks, was celibate but not necessarily in Holy Orders. As the difficulty of hearing Mass at the more isolated monasteries became a problem, abbots tended to become priests. They were normally chosen by the monks of the abbey from their own number and confirmed by the bishop. When the monasteries gained freedom from episcopal jurisdiction, the confirmation came directly from the Pope. Abbots were chosen on the basis of their learning and humility so as to be model instructors in doctrine and obedience. By the second half of the fourteenth century, there are stories of abbots living and dressing sumptuously and hunting, an activity repeatedly proscribed for those in the religious life. Thus when the narrator of the General Prologue says the pilgrim monk is "A manly man, to been an abbot able" (I, 167), there is irony with regard to the pilgrim, who sees the rule of St. Benedict as outdated, and satire of the reputed behavior of some real abbots. Indeed, the whole portrait of the pilgrim monk (I, 165-207) may be a catalogue of contemporary abuses including violations of the monastic vows of poverty, stability, and even chastity. (See ***monk***.)

Abraham. The first of the great Jewish patriarchs (Gen. 11-25). God promised Abraham that he would be the father of a great and numerous progeny. Although his wife Sarah did not conceive until late in life, Abraham remained faithful. After the birth of his son ***Isaac***, God again tested Abraham by commanding him to sacrifice his only son. God, however, interrupted the sacrifice as reward for Abraham's staunch fidelity. Thus Abraham's absolute trust in God became the basis for the first covenant between Jehovah and His "chosen people", and Abraham became the "father" of his people and the source of Hebrew religion. His designation as "Father of the Jews" was, however, not always a title of honor when used in the anti-Semitic context of the fourteenth century.

Absalon, Absolon. The third son of Kind ***David***, Absolom was renowned for his flowing hair and almost feminine beauty. He rebelled against his father, largely because of David's preferment of his first-born, Amnon. Absolom killed Amnon, fled, and led an unsuccessful insurrection. Fleeing in a rout, Absolom caught his hair in a tree and was slain by David's general, Joab, leading to David's pathetic lament for his wayward, but beloved, son. (2 Sam. 13-18) (See ***scripture***.)

absolucio(u)n. The remission of sin or the punishment due to sin in the sacrament of ***Penance*** administered by a priest. There was a long controversy, including much commentary by the scholastic philosophers, about the power of a priest to forgive sin. The issue was resolved, for the later Middle Ages, by Thomas Aquinas's conclusion that God in fact forgives the sin through the necessary ministration of the priest as His vicar or representative. Absolution is, however, conditional upon the penitent's confession of his sins, true sorrow for them, purpose of amendment, and satisfaction through prayer, almsgiving, and other penitential acts. (See ***sacrement***.)

abstinence, abstynence (also **Abstinaunce, Abstynaunce** as a personification). In a general sense, abstinence is the refraining from any sinful activity or from lawful activity for penitential purposes. More specifically, however, it refers to dietary prohibitions on specified days or during specified seasons, usually from the eating of meat. Dietary restrictions were familiar from the Hebrew practice, *e.g.* on the Day of Atonement (Lev. 16:29 ff.), and ***fasting*** and abstinence were common in the early Church in imitation of Christ's forty days in the desert (Matt. 4:1-11; Luke 4:1-13) and to appease God's justice as a consequence of the Fall of Adam and Eve.

Abstinence proper, the refraining from meat, was imposed on all Fridays according to repeated papal decrees as early as Nicholas I (858-867) and Innocent III (1198-1216). In addition, abstinence was required as early as the seventh century by Gregory I on weekdays in the seasons of Lent and Advent as well as other specified days, such as the days preceding religious feasts. Abstinence was, then, not only the rule of life for monastics, but a familiar fact of life for all Christians.

accidie. The deadly sin of sloth. It is more of a disposition than a specific action, an aversion to the difficulty of living an upright life, a kind of spiritual laziness in the face of the obligations of the Christian life, and is therefore directly opposed to the active virtue of ***charity***, which enjoins good works. Derived from the Latin "acedia", it is perhaps best described as a lack of will or commitment and, as such, can be the source of serious sins. (See ***deedly synnes***.)

Achitofel. The haughty counselor of Absolom (***Absalon***) in his rebellion against his father King ***David***. When the insurrection was routed, Achitophel committed suicide. (See ***scripture***.)

Adam. The first man and the father of the human race. In Genesis the name can refer to mankind in general, but was ordinarily applied to the individual first man. His fall from original innocence and righteousness changed the terms of human existence. The guilt of his sin, original sin, was imputed to all his progeny and could be removed only by Baptism (***Baptesme***). His sin, and Eve's, separated the human race from salvation until ***Redemption*** by ***Christ***, and thus accounts for the fallen and weakened moral state in which mankind lives as well as the adversities that flesh is heir to. (Gen. 1-2) (See ***scripture***.)

Aleyn. Alanus de Insulis (c. 1120-1202/3). Also called Alan of Lille and Alain de Lille, renowned as the "doctor universalis" for his mastery of the liberal arts and sometimes considered the father of systematic theology. His major works, *De Planctu Naturae* (*The Pleynt of Kind*, 1160-75) and the *Anticlandianus* (1182-3), emphasize the connection that Nature provides between God and man, but still insist upon the necessity of redemptive grace for man's salvation. Although the *De Planctu*, a Boethian (***Boece***) dialogue between the poet and nature, was more broadly known and cited in the fourteenth century, the *Anticlandianus* is a longer, more systematic, though allegorical, account of how Reason and Prudence use Theology as a guide to ***Faith*** and the reconstruction of the Golden Age. Most significant is Aleyn's insistence that Nature must be elevated by Grace to be efficacious.

Alma Redemptoris. A musical composition in praise of Mary (***Marie, Seinte***) as the mother of the Redeemer by Hermanus Contractus (1013-54). It was first sung as one of the Marian antiphons at the end of the office of Compline from the beginning of the liturgical season of Advent, beginning roughly four weeks before Christmas, until the Feast of the Purification on February 2. Later it was sung as an independent hymn and became associated with the Feast of the Assumption of Mary on August 15.

almes, almesse, almus(-dede). In the Hebrew Scriptures alms were substantive aid given to the poor, required by the Law, and bringing God's favor on the giver. In the Christian ***Scriptures***, alms are foundational in that they spring from Christian love and compassion. From the Greek word for "pity", they are enjoined from ***John the Baptist*** (Luke 3:11) through ***St. Paul*** (Rom. 15:25-28; 1 Cor. 16:1; 2 Cor. 8-9). Fundamentally related to our stewardship of material goods, they are a central Christian duty as well as a penitential act. Thomas Aquinas saw almsgiving as the principal work of mercy. Although alms are material in nature, theologians emphasized the primacy of the charitable intention and the enhancement of the unity of Christians. Mendicant orders had the right, with proper approval, to solicit alms and depended upon them for survival. (See ***frere***.)

Ambrose, Seint. St. Ambrose (339-397), Father and Doctor of the Church and Bishop of Milan (374), came from a wealthy family and was well educated in Rome. He was a man of public affairs as well as a theologian, insisting on the subjection of Emperors to the moral law of the Church. He was a scriptural scholar, an early devotee of allegorical interpretation of

Scripture and a formidable opponent of contemporary heretics, especially Arians. (See ***heresye***.)

amendement. Although there is a general meaning of reform, in a religious sense amendment is the correction of the spiritual life, a turning away from sin and the things of this world towards God and salvation. Along with ***confession***, ***contrition***, and satisfaction for sins committed, it is an essential condition for the granting of ***absolution*** in the sacrament of ***Penance***.

angel, aungel(l). Pure spirits whose role is to serve and praise God. The term comes from the Greek word for messenger, and their function was frequently seen to be intermediary between God and man. Although spiritual creatures, they are reported in the Christian ***Scriptures*** as taking human form in their dealings with man. From Gregory the Great (c. 540-604) to Bernard of Clairvaux (d. 1153) there was a tendency toward a cult of angels, St. Bernard especially noting the idea of the "guardian angel" for individual Christians. Medieval Christianity developed an elaborate angelology furthering the philosophical speculations of the scholastic philosophers, who were more interested in their nature than in the cult. The Fourth Lateran Council (1215) decreed that angels were pure spirits created before the material world. There emerged descriptions of elaborate duties and hierarchies based on traditions that had persisted from at least the fourth century. Thus, there were nine "choirs" of angels: five from ***St. Paul*** (virtues, powers, principalities, dominations, and thrones) plus angels, archangels, cherubim and seraphim.

Satan (***Sathan***) was the leader of the fallen angels who, before the creation of man, rebelled against God and were expelled from heaven and condemned to eternal ***damnation***.

Angelus ad Virginem. A religious song based on the Annunciation to Mary by the angel Gabriel that she would be the mother of Christ (Luke 1:26-38). It is listed as part of Nicholas's repertoire in the "Miller's Tale", and identifies him more certainly with learning than with religion since the song was often sung in collegiate institutions after Compline; it did not achieve liturgical status as a hymn until the fifteenth century. Nevertheless, it is difficult to escape the irony of associating this praise of the Virgin with Nicholas, who will soon seduce the willing Alison. The song is also thematically related to the "Magnificat", Mary's speech to her cousin

Elizabeth regarding the angel's message, a motif common in the later Middle Ages, which predicts the destruction of the powerful and the exaltation of the humble. If we are expected to call this to mind, the association with Nicholas is, once again, ironic. (See ***Marie, Seinte***.)

anger, angre. One of the seven deadly sins, anger is a disposition towards ill will or indignation which can become seriously sinful when not kept under control. Of course, anger can be righteous when its object is sin or injustice, but when it is unfounded, or exceeds rational proportions, or is directed against an undeserving recipient, it is contrary to moral law as a sin of excess. (See ***deedly synnes***.)

Anne, Seint. The mother of the Blessed Virgin Mary and husband of St. Joachim, St. Anne is not actually a Scriptural figure. Her story derives from the *Protoevangelium of James* and other apocryphal writing of the late second century. The cult of Anne grew as devotion to Mary increased and, although churches were erected in her honor from the sixth century, she did not really become popular in Europe until the height of devotion to Mary in the fourteenth century.

annueleer. A priest (***prest***), ordinarily associated with a religious establishment called a *chaunterie* (therefore, sometimes called a "chantry priest"), who celebrated commemorative masses for the dead, usually on an annual basis. The chaunterie was supported by gifts, usually in the form of endowments, from relatives or patrons of the deceased. Such masses of remembrance and petition for the soul of the departed might be offered more frequently, for example the "month's mind" mass. Especially among the aristocracy and the more privileged classes endowments were provided to support annual observation in perpetuity.

anoynt(en). To rub or pour oil for religious or ceremonial purposes. Anointing is associated with the coronation of kings and the consecration of bishops, though it could be used in more generalized secular contexts. Anointing was part of the administration of the ***sacraments*** of Baptism (***Baptesme***), Confirmation, and Holy Orders. The most specific kind of anointing was of the five senses in the sacrament of Extreme Unction, which was believed to restore spiritual, and sometimes physical, health to those in danger of death. Its sacramentality was only rigorously defined at the Council of Trent (1545), but it had long been the practice of the Church: the earliest reference to it is in the Venerable Bede (735) and it had received its name by the end of the twelfth century.

Anselm, Seint. St. Anselm (1033-1109) was a Doctor of the Church and Archbishop of ***Canterbury***. He became a monk in 1060, but was prominent in public affairs, highly regarded among the great and powerful including William the Conqueror. A strong advocate of papal authority, he opposed the secular appointment of bishops. Although overshadowed by successors, he was an early scholastic philosopher, whose best-known contribution is his "ontological proof" for the existence of God:
1. God is "that which nothing greater can be thought".
2. What exists in reality is greater than that which exists in the mind.
3. Therefore, God exists in reality.

(See ***Seint***.)

Antechirst. An antithesis or imitation or nemesis of ***Christ***. St. John in his Epistles (1 John 2:18; 1 John 4:3) speaks as if many existed in fact or potentially. The Antichrist sometimes seems to be a generalized seducer away from the faith (2 John 7). In some instances he is seen as coming at the last hour as the end of the world approaches; in others he seems already to exist in the world, perhaps in many forms. He has been identified with many of the beasts described in the Book of Revelation: the red dragon, the beast with seven heads, the beast like a lamb that speaks like a dragon. A version of the Antichrist appears in St. Paul (2 Thess.2) as the man of sin who will precede the triumph of the Lord. Although he may be a threatening power that lurks in the world, he is most often seen as a dangerous and disruptive force that will appear in the last days before the second coming of Christ. (See ***scripture***.)

Antony, Seint. St. Anthony of the Desert is traditionally seen as the founder of Christian monasticism. Born in the middle of the third century, he lived in huts, which attracted a few ascetic disciples, until about 270, when he withdrew entirely to live in a tomb near his native village of Coma except for visits to other ascetics for instruction. Eventually, he removed himself to an old fort on the East bank of the Nile where he lived in solitude for twenty years despite pleas of pilgrims to see him. In 305 he emerged as vigorous as when he had gone into seclusion. After spending five or six years instructing the loose community of monks that had sprung up around him, he withdrew to the desert between the Nile and the Red Sea to spend the last forty years of his life in total seclusion. A monastic rule, orally transmitted, is attributed to him, though his own life was rather eremitic. He is not to be confused with St. Anthony of Padua (1195-1231), a Franciscan ***Canon Regular***—preacher, miracle worker, and associate of St. Francis of Assisi.

Apocalips(e). The Book of Revelation, the last book of the Bible. Dealing with the "end times", it is a strange kind of visionary literature popular during the first century before and after Christ. At one time or another attributed to St. John, the Apostle beloved of Jesus, or to St. John the Evangelist, its visions are so bizarre that it was assigned allegorical interpretations as early as the second century by Clement of Alexandria and Origen. Its authorship has been disputed since the third century. Its account of visions, fanciful and horrible, that will precede the second coming of Christ, has long fascinated scholars and laymen. Its main teaching is that, in the end, evil will be punished and Christ will come in glory to vindicate the righteous. (See ***scripture***.)

apostel, apostle. "One who is sent forth" rather as a delegate than a messenger. Ordinarily it refers to the twelve disciples most closely associated with Jesus and his teaching mission, who were sent forth to spread the word after Christ's Ascension. They are specially named and appointed to this mission in all three of the synoptic Gospels: Peter, John, James the Greater, James the Less, Thaddeus, Bartholomew, Thomas, Philip, Simon the Zealot, Levi, Andrew, and ***Judas*** Iscariot (Luke 6:13; Matt. 10:1-15; Mark 3:14). Bishops are the successors of the Apostles in an unbroken line and retain the teaching authority granted to the Apostles. This is the basis of episcopal authority in the Medieval Church.

appetit, appetyt. A natural inclination or tendency. Sense appetite is a natural drive towards the gratification of the senses. Although there are intellectual appetites with intellectual objects or goals, the term usually refers to the sensual. Appetites like hunger and thirst can be good, but must be kept under rational control so as not to come into conflict with the will. Submission to excesses of the sensual appetites is the source of sins of the flesh like gluttony, drunkenness, and sexual misconduct. These cravings are, however, seen as natural and human, and the sins that flow therefrom, though frequently condemned by preachers motivated by either morality or avarice, are normally the most understandable and benign.

archaungell. Although a special role for archangels is suggested by St. Paul (1 Thess. 4:16), their exact distinctions are not clear in ***Scripture***, where only Raphael, Gabriel, and Michael are mentioned by name.

Assuer(e), (us). Assuer is most often identified as the husband of *Esther* (Esther 1:17). An elusive figure, he seems sometimes (Esther 4:16) to be Xerxes, the King of Persia. Elsewhere (Tob. 14:4) he seems to be the King of Media who conquered Assyria with Nebuchadnezzar (***Nabugodonosor***). Although the historical identifications are highly conjectural, Assuer is the type of the arrogant pagan monarch.

astrologien. An astronomer, a scientific student of the cosmos, or an astrologer, a student of the influence of the cosmos (the positioning of the heavenly bodies) affects the course of human life. (See ***astrologye***.)

ASTROLOGYE. Astrologye and the related terms ***astrologien*** and ***astromye*** refer to the study of celestial bodies and their effects on the affairs of human beings. Although possessed of a strictly secular or scientific sense, they have religious significance insofar as they challenge doctrines concerning ***fate***, free will (***fredom***), and Divine Providence (***purveaunce***), concerns which are very common in Chaucer and therefore deserving of special attention.

It is not surprising to find, throughout history and across the globe, the belief that heavenly bodies influence human behavior. Interest in the effects of the stars, and later of the sun, moon, and planets, dates from about 3000 B.C.E. in the Babylonian Empire. Already in these Euphratean civilizations a dual application of the term "astrology" to a practical science and a magical art had begun to appear. Later the distinction was made explicit as astrology was divided into "natural astrology", which inquired into the motions of the heavenly bodies, and "judicial astrology", which attempted to explain the effects of heavenly arrangements and motions on human affairs. The former was predictive in the sense that it tried to plot, by means of celestial correspondences, the occurrence of natural phenomena such as floods, earthquakes, and eclipses. The latter extended the predictive pretensions of the "science" to human experience and moral behavior, eventually including putatively precise mechanisms like horoscopes. Thus from very early on the dual aspect of astrology was apparent.

Astrology was transmitted from the ancient Near East to fourth-century B.C.E. Greece, pre-Christian Rome, and Hellenistic Egypt. The most revered early treatises on astrology were Ptolemy's *Almagest* and *Tetrabiblion*, the former a rather conservative scientific exegesis, the latter a more fanciful inquiry into "judicial astrology". Teachings of the more occult sort found receptive audiences in the Stoics because of their disposition towards fatalism, and in the Pythagoreans because of their fascination with the numerical. Early Church Fathers were vigorous in their condemnation of "judicial astrology" because of its tendency to assert a natural determinism (***fate***), which thwarted Divine Providence (***purveaunce***) and contradicted free will (***fredom***). (Even the third-century neo-Platonist Plotinus insisted that the stars were merely signs rather than causes of things.) Augustine was perhaps the most prominent figure to adduce "the argument of the twins" to refute the predictive capacity of astrology: if twins, born at almost precisely the same time, could differ so much from each other, how could the positions of celestial bodies at their birth have had a determinative influence? But Augustine was not alone in his criticisms. Basil the Great, John of Damascus, and the Council of Toledo all condemned the magical and fatalistic contentions of astrology. It was Isidore of Seville, in the seventh century, who first made the distinction between "natural" and "judicial" astrology and dismissed the latter. However, the modern distinction between astrology and astronomy was not clearly established until the sixteenth century.

Despite these early condemnations, astrology was reintroduced as a major intellectual force in the later Middle Ages by Arab scholars. Translations of Ptolemy into Arabic, begun in the eighth century, found their way into the later Medieval tradition through the Moorish universities at Cordoba and Toledo in the eleventh and twelfth centuries. Once again Christian resistance was readily apparent in twelfth-century rebuttals by Gratian (*Decretum*), John of Salisbury, and Hugh of St. Victor (*Didascalion*). And later, Bishop Etienne Tempier prohibited the teaching of astrological determinism at the University of Paris.

Repudiation of the more occult and fatalistic forms of astrology was not, however, uniform. Thirteenth-century scholastic philosophers, influenced by Aristotle's descriptions of motion, especially that of a Prime Mover that set into effect all consequent motions, found varying degrees of plausibility in astral effects on human events and actions. In accepting Aristotle, they became more receptive to at least the more conservative claims of Ptolemy that the heavens had a profound impact on human nature and destiny. Still, the mixture of Christianity and the "judicial" forms of astrology was a rather uneasy one. Although Roger Bacon may have been more sympathetic than most, many scholastic philosophers inclined towards a limited acceptance. Albertus Magnus subscribed to many Ptolemaic ideas, but stopped short of full-blown determinism by asserting the ultimate freedom of the human will. There developed an array of accommodations between the effects that the stars could have on human character and behavior, and the ultimate realities of free will and Divine Providence. The clearest exposition of a balanced and orthodox view in later fourteenth-century England is the explanation by Genius in John Gower's *Confessio Amantis* (VII, 633-1236). And Gower was Chaucer's contemporary and sometime friend.

Nevertheless, ambiguities remained and were reflected in popular beliefs and public practices. Indeed, court astrologers survived, at least on the continent, through the fourteenth century. The most authoritative (and balanced) philosophical indictment of superstitious astrology is by St. Thomas Aquinas, who distinguished clearly between general influence and determinism. Regardless, more simplistic views persisted on the fringes of the intellectual life and in the popular imagination.

Chaucer's understanding of astrology was that of an unusually well-informed layman rather than that of the specialist or philosopher. He was certainly no devotee of "judicial astrology" although he was well aware of its persistence. His "Treatise on the Astrolabe", written by his own account for his ten-year-old son Lewis, is a didactic exposition on the uses of the astrolabe, the main Medieval instrument for astronomical observation and calculation; the explanation is pedagogically designed for his young reader. Yet it is one of the earliest disquisitions in English on a scientific subject and, in its practical turn of mind, it is an accurate, if dry, explanation of the functions of the instrument in "natural astrology", rather what we might call basic astronomy.

Chaucer's knowledge of "natural astrology" is also apparent in the flight of the eagle in the *House of Fame*, Troilus's perspective from the eighth sphere in *Troilus and Criseyde*, and various indications of time and season throughout the *Canterbury Tales*—from the position of the sun in the "Ram" (Aries, the first of the twelve signs of the zodiac into which astrologers divided the visible heavens) to the specification of the time of day in the Prologue to the "Parson's Tale". Although Chaucer's knowledge is relatively extensive for a layman, his references to astrological phenomena, *in propria persona*, are generally limited to observations of this "natural" sort. Some critics (*e.g.*, Ann W. Astell and J.D. North) see these references, especially in the *Canterbury Tales*, to be so ubiquitous as to have structural significance for the work as a whole. Certainly it is common for Chaucer to identify times of year or times of day by astrological references, but this practice does not imply acceptance of "judicial astrology".

Chaucer was aware of the occult claims of the astrological arts, as indicated, for example, by the mention of the Wife of Bath's horoscope. But acceptance of such claims is rather the province of the pagan or pre-Christian environments as in *Troilus and Criseyde*, the "Knight's Tale", or the "Man of Law's Tale", or of shady characters such as Nicholas in the "Miller's Tale" or the Clerk of Orleans in the "Franklin's Tale". In fact, the Franklin is careful to note that such beliefs are only appropriate to the benighted pre-Christian past. Thus, "judicial astrology" seems to be consistently associated with ignorance, fraud, or deviance.

FURTHER READING: Walter Clyde Curry, *Chaucer and the Mediaeval Sciences* (New York, London: Oxford University Press, 1926; rev. New York: Barnes and Noble, 1960); Theodore Otto Wedel, *The Medieval Attitude Toward Astrology* (New Haven: Yale University Press, 1920; rpt. Hamden, CT: Archon Books, 1968); Chauncey Wood, *Chaucer and the Country of the Stars* (Princeton: Princeton University Press, 1970); John David North, *Chaucer's Universe* (New York: Oxford University Press, 1988); Ann W. Astell, *Chaucer and the Universe of Learning* (Ithaca, NY: Cornell University Press, 1996).

astromye. The study of heavenly bodies or cosmology, but, more ominously, the study of the influence of heavenly bodies on the affairs of human beings. In the first sense, astromye is what we would call astronomy. In the second sense it was sometimes seen as determinative of human events, what we would call astrology, and was in conflict with orthodox Christian doctrine. (See ***astrologye***.)

attricioun. In general usage, a moderate form of repentance. In a strictly religious sense, however, it is sorrow for sin occasioned not by love of God or regret for having offended Him, but rather by the fear of the loss of ***salvation*** or of eternal punishment in hell. Sometimes called "imperfect ***contrition***", it was sufficient for ***absolution*** within the ***sacrament*** of ***Penance*** administered by a priest, but not sufficient for forgiveness absent formal reception of the sacrament. "Perfect contrition" could immediately effect forgiveness and allow salvation in the event that the person died before receiving the sacrament.

Augustyn, Austyn. St. Augustine of Hippo (354-430), author of the *Confessions*, *The City of God*, and a wealth of other treatises and commentaries, was born of a Christian mother and a pagan father in the Roman province of Africa. He rose to prominence as a teacher of rhetoric in Rome and Milan, converted to Christianity, reluctantly accepted consecration as a bishop, and became perhaps the single most influential Christian author in the West during the first millennium and well into the second. Influenced by ***St. Ambrose***, he is the earliest figure to comment extensively on the allegorical exegesis of ***Scripture***, and his commentary on Genesis strongly influenced in this regard both secular and religious writing. To him is attributed the monastic ***rule*** of the Augustinians one of the four major monastic orders of the Middle Ages, though no such rule was formally written by St. Augustine and it probably developed through an oral tradition based on other writings. (See ***Augustyns***)

St. Augustine of Canterbury (d. c. 605), although not mentioned by Chaucer, was a Benedictine ***monk*** sent from Rome by Pope Gregory the Great in 597 to evangelize the Saxons of England. Disheartened by real and anticipated hardships, Augustine's missionary band gave up en route, and Augustine returned to Rome. (Pilgrimages to Canterbury had their vicissitudes long before Chaucer's time.) He was, however, persuaded by the Pope to press on to England and became the first archbishop of Canterbury, thereby remotely setting the stage for the martyrdom of Becket and the *Canterbury Tales*.

Augustyns. One of the four major orders of Medieval monasticism. Although ***St. Augustine*** of Hippo lived "as a monk" even in his episcopal palace, he was not the founder of an ***order***. Rather it is his "***rule***", roughed out in his Letter 211 (to a community of women) and his Sermons 355 and 356 (titled "De Vita et Moribus Clericorum Suorum"), that became a model for a large number of independent monasteries over the several hundred years following his death (430 C.E.). His "rule" enjoined poverty, prayer, self-denial, and work as the fundamental ingredients of monastic life. During his lifetime monasticism was widespread and diverse; the emergence of his "rule" had an ordering effect, although there is no true monastic "rule", strictly speaking, until St. Benedict (***Beneit***). (See ***monk***.)

Austyn. See ***Augustyn***.

avarice, avaryce. The deadly sin of greed or covetousness. It is an inordinate desire for money or possessions or a kind of miserliness. The problem it poses as a moral disposition is that it diverts us from spiritual goals and is especially destructive of Christian charity (***charite***). Under the general heading of this capital sin, Chaucer's Parson distinguishes between avarice proper, the desire to keep things without need, and covetousness (***covetise***), the desire to have what belongs to another. In the fourteenth century avarice was often particularly associated, in satire and the popular imagination, with the Church hierarchy, who apparently lived in aristocratic splendor, as well as, ironically, with ***monks*** and friars (***frere***), who had taken vows of poverty and whose lives were supposed to embody the renunciation of material things. (See ***deedly synnes***.)

Ave Marie. The "Salutation of the Blessed Virgin", a prayer known and said from very early Christian times and especially in vogue during the zenith of veneration of Mary in the fourteenth century. The first half of the prayer is a combination of the Angel Gabriel's greeting to Mary at the Annunciation (Luke 1:38) and St. Elizabeth's greeting to Mary (Luke 1:42). The second half of the prayer was added later and indeed not officially sanctioned until the Council of Trent (1545).

The first half became embedded in monastic prayers, and, by the late twelfth century the Bishop of Paris prescribed that this prayer, along with the Lord's Prayer and the Apostles' Creed, be known by the laity. This prescription was reinforced by the Synod of Durham (1217). The increasing popularity of the prayer paralleled increased devotion to Mary. The *Ancrene Riwle* (*Rule of the Anchoresses*, pre-1200) enjoined genuflection or prostration with each recitation of the prayer. Nevertheless, controversies existed about whether it was a prayer at all or rather a simple greeting until the addition of the petition, in the second half of the prayer, to "pray for us sinners now and at the hour of our death". In any case, the ubiquity of the prayer of salutation is a sign of the fundamental role of Mary in fourteenth century devotional life. (See ***Marie, Seinte***.)

aventure. Although this word has many general impositions of chance, risk, mishap, exploit, adventure, or even simply an event, it takes on religious significance when it is used to indicate fortune or chance as determinants of the course of human life in the controversies over the operations of fate, free will, predestination, and God's foreknowledge of human events. (See ***fate, fortune***.)

avouterie, avouterye, avowtrie, avoutrye. In its primary imposition it is adultery in the familiar sense—sexual intercourse in which one or both parties are married to someone else. This is the sense in which it is used by January in the "Merchant's Tale" when he disingenuously worries that he will fall into adultery unless he takes a young wife (IV, 1431-36). The Parson, citing ***Matthew*** and ***Augustine***, also uses it in this sense under the category of "lechery" in his Tale. He identifies its evil as a breaking of faith with God and with one's spouse, as the etymology of the word would indicate (X, 840 ff.). Consistent with Medieval Christian teaching, the Parson also identifies as adulterous the desire for another man's wife and, citing St. Jerome (***Jeremie***), even sexual intercourse between husband and wife when the only purpose is gratification of the flesh (X, 904 ff.). (See ***deedly synnes***.)

Balthasar. Belshazzar (Dan. 5), the son of Nebuchadnezzar (***Nabugodonosor***), and the last king of Babylon. Nebuchadnezzar's sacred vessels were used by Belshezzar's wives and concubines during his last feast. During the feast, a hand writes on the wall "Mane, Thecel, Phares" (A.V.: "Mene, Tekel, Peres."). The king's counselors are not able to interpret the handwriting on the wall, but Daniel, already renowned as a seer, is called and predicts defeat and subjugation by the Persians and Medes. More detail, essentially compatible with the Book of Daniel, is added by Herodotus and Xenophon, but those writers would have been unavailable to Chaucer.

Baptesme. Baptism, the ***sacrament*** of regeneration which frees human beings from the guilt of original (Adam's) sin, as opposed to ***Penance***, the sacrament of resuscitation, which frees human beings from the guilt of actual (personal) sin. Baptism incorporates one into the Christian community by the use of water, a washing that cleanses from sin, and by invocation of the Holy Spirit.

Baptist. See ***John the Baptist, Seint***

Basilie. St. Basil the Great (329-379) was Bishop of Caesarea and the great opponent of the Eastern heresies. He wrote prolifically if not profoundly, especially homilies and apologetics directed against figures such as Eunomius and the Eastern Arians. St. Basil was renowned for his ascetic life. His mass of dogmatic and exegetical writings focus largely on the doctrine of the Trinity (***trinite***) and, because of his antagonism to the Arians, on the divinity of ***Christ***. Generally regarded as a staunch defender of orthodoxy.

bedes, bedis. Originally simply prayers, or the "beadsman", who by vocation and for remuneration prayed for the intentions of others. More importantly, bedes referred to a set of beads strung together; such counters had been used in many religions from ancient times. Beads in the sense of "rosary beads" are first noted in 1351, although their use had been increasing in popularity from the twelfth century. Originally sets were called paternosters because the Our Father was the prayer said on each bead of a standard set. During the twelfth century, the Ave Maria largely supplanted the Our Father in bead-saying, and a standard set included "counters" for 150 Aves and 15 Our Fathers. (Sets for the laity were generally one-third size.) Beads were long attributed to St. Dominic (c. 1170-1221) though their use clearly antedates him. The term rosary for beads came from "rosarium", a garden of roses, but was apparently not yet in use in Chaucer's lifetime.

begger(e). Either a poor person or a mendicant. The mendicant orders of friars (***frere***) were empowered to beg by the local ecclesiastical authority, and their "begging" was accompanied with admonitory sermons. There was a responsibility on the part of the laity to give alms to friars as these gifts were their only means of support. The responsibility extended, however, to other beggars because of the general duty to give alms to the poor as an act of charity. Naturally, the begging of the friars was vulnerable to widespread abuse, and the disingenuous friar was a familiar object of satire in the fourteenth century. The corruption of friars was all the more reprehensible because of their vow of poverty.

Belial. A synonym for Satan, the Prince of Darkness, who is contrasted with ***Christ***, the Prince of Light (2 Cor. 6:15). In the Hebrew Bible, Belial is not a name but rather means "wickedness".

Benedight, Beneit. St. Benedict of Narsia (c. 480-543) was probably the most influential figure in the history of monasticism. From a somewhat sophisticated Roman family, he withdrew to solitude, founding twelve monasteries and living in the thirteenth. He has been honored as the patriarch of monasticism since the eighth century. At Monte Cassino in about 530 he established his famous "rule", whose introduction and propagation changed the face of monasticism in the Western Church. The rule, designed for cenobites, monks living in community, rather than anchorites, solitaries, emphasized work, prayer, and a balanced and sensible regimen of fasting and self-denial. The rule was an elaborate but sensible guide to Christian monastic life, enabling men to join together to live a simple but rigorous Christian life.

The Benedictines declined during the thirteenth through fifteenth centuries, in part because of the affluence which their hard work and simple lives produced. Wealth nourished a tendency towards elaborate church building and decoration and lavish hospitality. In such circumstances, they were vulnerable to corruption, suffered from comparison with the dynamism of the emerging mendicant orders, and declined in numbers.

Their accomplishments, however, were many, and attempts at reform like that by the Cistercians, notably ***St. Bernard*** of Clairvaux, periodically revivified the order. (See ***monk***.)

Bernard, Seint. St. Bernard of Clairvaux (1090-1153) was perhaps the most powerful and effective reformer of the Benedictine order. He engaged in controversy with the Benedictines at Cluny (Cluniacs), themselves a reforming group founded in the tenth century who effected a modest reform, though controversy between the Cluniacs and Bernard's more austere Cistercians continued. The Cistercians distinguished themselves with their white habits (white monks) as opposed to the Cluniacs, who wore black. Bernard was a proponent of a return to the rigor of the original rule of St. Benedict and resisted the rationalism of the Cluniacs. He was a model of orthodoxy, resistant to secular authority as well as to official Church pressure. He was a powerful force in organizing Benedictine houses into a confederation rather than as separate foundations. (See ***monk***.)

Bethulia, Bethulie. The town defended by Judith against the attack of Holofernes' (***Oloferne***) host. It became symbolic of Jerusalem.

Bible. The Holy ***Scripture***, both Hebrew and Christian, divided into the Old Testament and the New. It was revered as the revealed Word of God, and provided a treasury of *exempla*, exemplary lessons, for the preaching of friars (***frere***) and parish priests (***parson***, ***prest***) as well as summoners (***sumnour***) and ***pardoners***. From the second century onward there was controversy about whether Biblical accounts were to be understood literally or allegorically. In any case, Scriptural exegesis was a major form of religious writing for the Fathers and Doctors of the Church. A fourteenth-century translation into English is attributed to the heretical John Wyclif (d. 1384) though it was probably not completed until after his death. (See ***scripture***, ***Lollere***.)

bigamye. Literally the circumstance of having two mates, but the word assumed various meanings in the Middle Ages. It could refer to two or more simultaneous marriages, two or more serial marriages, or marriage by someone in Holy Orders. Church law against bigamy was strict though not always uniformly applied or enforced. The death of a spouse, for example, usually allowed a second marriage, but not always entry into Holy Orders.

bisshop. The almost monarchical ruler of a sub-division, usually geographical, of the Church. Bishops derived their powers by virtue of the doctrine of apostolic succession, which held that they were the successors as teachers and authorities in a direct line from the Apostles. They ruled, subject only to the authority of the Pope, over the spiritual and administrative affairs in their diocese. Because of their power, and many actual abuses of their position, they were often seen by the ordinary laity as rich, regal, and arbitrary, though their right to office and authority was rarely questioned, having been established as the familiar organization of Church affairs since at least the second century when some system of governance became required by the growing number of Christians.

blak (monkes). Benedictines, especially Cluniacs, who wore a black habit, as opposed to the reformer Cistercians, who wore a white habit. (See ***monk***.)

blasphemynge. Cursing, mocking, or defying God. Blasphemy is different from heresy in that it is not necessarily inconsistent with orthodoxy of faith. It is rather defiance by word or action both of God Himself and of a wide range of religious figures and institutions. It could extend from the indictment of God as a deceiver to such extended forms as the assertion that ***fate*** rules men's lives rather than Divine Providence, and it could be committed in thought as well as in deed. The definition became so broad that heresies came to be thought of as a form of blasphemy insofar as they were an inappropriate challenge to God's truths. Blasphemy was a civil as well as a religious offense though it was usually punished in the ecclesiastical courts (***Court Cristien***). (See ***heresye***.)

blisful(l), blissful. Verbal, adjectival, adverbial, and compound variants of this word abound. In general, it refers to a condition of rapture or joy, particularly that associated with heavenly salvation. To bliss something is to sanctify it, to make it holy, to set it apart. Although applied to human joy as well as sanctification, its religious sense implies beatific transformation. A "blisful ***martir***" certainly lives with God in heaven.

Boece. Anicius Manilius Severinus Boethius (c. 480-524/6) came from a powerful Roman family and was early influenced by both Greek philosophy and Christian orthodoxy. Early political success brought on (apparently) vindictive charges of occultism, and he was imprisoned in 523 and executed between 524 and 526. Although many of his didactic works on the quadrivium (arithmetic, music, geometry, and astronomy) are not extant, his logical and theological treatises and translations made him the primary source of Aristotle for the Middle Ages, as a founder of the attempt to accommodate Christianity with ancient philosophy that saw its culmination in Aquinas. His most influential work, *The Consolation of Philosophy*, written while in prison, is primarily a dialogue with the allegorical figure of Philosophy; based on the ideas of Plato, Aristotle, Cicero, Augustine, and others, deals with the problems of evil, ***fate***, foreknowledge (***forknowynge***), and free will (***fredom***). Translated by Chaucer, *The Consolation* was "required reading" in the fourteenth century. (See ***purveaunce***.)

Bradwardyn. Thomas Bradwardine (1290/1300-1349) was a fellow of Balliol College, a Doctor of Divinity at Merton College, and Chancellor of Oxford University. He became chaplain and confessor to Edward III and, in 1349, Archbishop of Canterbury. Forty days after his consecration he died of the plague. He wrote early treatises of natural philosophy on "motion". Strongly influenced by Augustine, Anselm, and especially Aquinas, he wrote his great metaphysical work, *De Causa Dei*, an attack on the "new Pelagians", perhaps contemporaries like William of Ockham. He argued that human free will is not entirely independent of divine causality, and he addressed the primacy of God's causality, the reality of man's free will *under grace*, and the problems of God's foreknowledge and future contingent events. The "doctor profundus", as he was called, was an acknowledged authority on the issue of reconciliation of foreknowledge and free will, which are so prominent in *Troilus and Criseyde* (esp. 960-1078) and the "Nun's Priest's Tale", where he is ranked in importance with Boethius and Augustine (VII, 3241-42). (See ***Boece.***)

bulle. A papal decree, so called because of the seal (bulla). Bulls opened with the Pope's name, title, and the purpose of the decree. They are usually known and referred to by the first words of the text (*e.g.* Bonaface VIII's *Unam sanctam*, 1302). Bulls were of general theological, moral, or disciplinary significance, and included political excommunications. They never dealt with private matters. Use of the term became so common that it eventually took on the broader meaning of any papal communication with a seal.

Canaan. Canaan's father, Ham, saw Noah naked in his drunkenness. His brothers, Shem and Japheth averted their eyes and put a cloak over him (Gen. 9:20-27). God cursed Canaan, as a descendant of Ham, and made him subservient to the heirs of Shem and Japheth.

Cananee (woman). The Canaanite woman came to Jesus, though unworthy because she was not a Jew, and appealed for the healing of her daughter. Because of her humility and faith Jesus granted her petition (Matt. 15:22-28).

Cane (of Galilee). Jesus attended a wedding feast at Cana in Galilee. When they ran out of wine, Jesus, at the request of his mother, changed six urns of water into wine (John 2:1-11). The story is both a sign of His reverence for Mary (she says only, quite simply, "They have no wine"), and an affirmation of marriage.

cano(u)n, chano(u)n. According to the early Church Fathers, a canon was a "rule of faith". Thus it was a precept or principle of the Church, such as the so-called "Apostolic canons", guidelines for orthodoxy which were according apostolic authority. It was also a sanctioned authoritative book, especially a book of the Bible. In this sense, it became associated with the "canon" of the Scriptures, the set of books officially established as authentic, inspired works.

Chaucer's uses of the term, however, generally refer to a clergyman, either in a religious order (a canon regular) or simply serving communally in a cathedral or major church (a canon secular). Ordinarily canons were members of a college of clerics whose primary function was worship at a cathedral or collegiate church. Canons flourished in the twelfth century and fell somewhere between parish priests and monks. They followed, to a greater or lesser degree, some loosely conceived version of the ***rule*** of ***St. Augustine***. Aquinas argued, ultimately prevailing in practice, that canons must be priests, though they ordinarily lived semi-monastic (Austin canons) lives or devoted themselves to worship (collegiate canons.) Thus, they were, or should have been, models of orthodoxy and devotion.

cardinal, cardynales. Cardinals were originally the rectors of the 28 *tituli*, private houses donated for the needs of the Church. By the end of the eleventh century, the title implied a superior rank, though not episcopal, there being cardinal bishops, priests, and deacons. By the end of the thirteenth century, they had their own treasury and shared papal revenues. Pope Nicholas II in 1059 named them papal electors in addition to their roles as papal assistants, envoys, and advisors. Their close association with the popes became a source of distrust and controversy, most notably in ***St. Bernard*** of Clairvaux's allegations that they were usurping the rightful power of the bishops.

Carmes. The Carmelites, one of the four great mendicant orders (***frere***), emerged from a semi-hermetic community established around Mount Carmel by St. Berthold about 1155. They led the contemplative life though leavened with preaching and works of charity. Their rule was written in 1209 and approved by Pope Honorius in 1226. The fall of the "crusader states" led to their migration to Cyprus and eventually Europe after 1238. They retained their lives of simplicity and devotion to the Blessed Virgin Mary. St. Simon Stock revised their rule in 1247 and allowed urban foundations that transformed them into communities much more resembling Franciscans and Dominicans than their solitary desert forebears. They declined during the fourteenth century and many were assimilated by the Dominicans.

ca(a)s. In a very general sense, a situation, circumstance, or occurrence, but especially associated, like ***aventure***, with events connected with the operations of ***fortune*** or ***fate***.

Caunterbury. Canterbury was an early settlement, as early as the second century B.C.E., that passed through several forms. After the Romans, Geoffrey of Monmouth cites a foundation of 950 A.D., though there was clearly a Saxon settlement in the middle of the fifth century and the Roman monk Augustine founded a monastery there in 597 to evangelize the Anglo-Saxons.

Because of the importance of ***Thomas*** a Becket, it became one of the most important *pilgrimage* sites of the latter Middle Ages, rivaling St. James Compostela in Spain, and even the Holy Land. Becket, Lord Chancellor (1155) of Henry II and fourteenth Archbishop of Canterbury (1161), fell out with Henry and was murdered, probably at Henry's direction or at least with his compliance, in 1170, in the Cathedral. A plethora of miracles was almost immediately attributed to Becket, and Canterbury became a site of intense religious activity and prime importance soon after his death. It became a symbol of principled resistance to the king and a type of the New Jerusalem.

Caym. Cain, the murderer of his brother, Abel (Gen. 4). The spelling is odd, but the name is paired by the Parson with Judas as examples of sinners who are beyond Redemption. Cain was a common Medieval example of the foulest kind of treachery and perfidy.

Cecile, Cecilie. St. Cecilia is the patron saint of music and the blind, though little is made of either in the "Second Nun's Tale", a life of St. Cecilia, which does emphasize the clarity of her spiritual vision and the power of her faith. Although the story of her martyrdom was a familiar one, the historical facts of her life are obscure. She was probably a Roman lady who became a Christian and, as in the "Second Nun's Tale", converted her husband. Her life and persecution are variously placed in the second century under Marcus Aurelius, in the third century under Alexander Severus or Diocletian, or in the fourth century as a victim of Julian the Apostate.

celerer. The ***monk*** in a religious community in charge of providing, keeping, and managing the foundation's stores or supplies, especially food. The duties of the cellarer often required that he be free to leave the confines of the monastery in order to secure the necessary provisions or to administer proprietary agricultural land. A monk in this office was also called an ***outridere***. Comparable duties were sometimes required in other communities such as collegiate churches where numbers of priests lived and worshipped together.

celle. Among many disparate meanings from "dwellings" to "walls", cell in a religious context refers to the austere room of a monk in a monastery, to any specific room or storeroom in a monastery, or to a subordinate ("branch") monastery. It implies a constricted or confined space. (See ***monk***.)

chalice. Any cup, but particularly the cup for the sacramental wine at Mass. As such it is one of the holy vessels for religious ritual and severe penalties were attached to the misuse or desecration of sacred vessels. Because of its association with ***Christ***, the meaning of the word extended to include sacrificial suffering, though Chaucer does not seem to use it in this sense. Chalices were ordinarily made of gold or silver and richly ornamented with gemtones as a sign of respect for their sacramental content, the blood of Christ.

chapel. A part of a cathedral or large church containing a separate altar usually with a separate dedication to a saint. It could also be a small church attached to a religious foundation such as a monastery or convent. "Lady Chapels", devoted to the Blessed Virgin (***Marie, Seinte***), and other specialized chapels became popular in the later Middle Ages and were either attached to or separate from a church, or even built into the homes and castles of the nobility.

chapel(l)eyn(e). A priest officiating in a public or private *chapel* or any clergyman who assisted a cleric of higher rank. Chaplains were characteristically assigned to monasteries, when members were not priests, and to convents of nuns (***nonne***) to say Mass and provide the sacraments. It could also denote a nun assigned to an ***abbess*** or ***prioress*** as an assistant or secretary.

chapitre. A heading or separate section within a book, chapters became associated with the passages from ***Scripture*** read at Mass or to monks during their meals.

The term also applied to an assembly of all members of a religious order or a cathedral, acting often as a legislative or advisory body. At monastic foundations, the chapter was presided over by the ***abbot*** or ***abbess*** (or prior or ***prioress***), while at collegiate churches and cathedrals, where their function was always more administrative, by a dean or provost.

Chapter also designated a session of an ecclesiastical court (***Court Cristien***), usually presided over by an archdeacon (***erchedeken***), to sit in judgment on matters of ecclesiastical law.

charite(e). Although charity has extended, secularized meanings, it is principally the Christian love which is at the heart of the message of the Gospels. One of the three theological virtues, with faith and hope, it is identified as the greatest of these by ***St. Paul*** (1 Cor.13:13) because it will survive into eternity when there is no longer any need for faith and hope. It is the pure, non-sensual love of God, a perfect, selfless love directed towards God. It is also enjoined upon Christians as their fundamental duty towards each other and the basis of the Christian life. Christ's formulation of charity (love of God, self, and neighbor in Luke 10:25-27) is mirrored by St. Paul's teaching of the necessity that faith "live" in charity (2 Cor. 9 and Gal. 6:6-10). Charity includes forgiveness and spiritual generosity and, by extension, material generosity like almsgiving.

It is a power or habit directly infused by God, therefore supernatural. Although its first object is God (pure love of God for His own sake), it is manifested in love for man both for his own sake and for God's sake. The practice of charity resulted in the flourishing of monasticism, mendicancy, and a variety of institutions such as hospitals.

chastite(e), chastyte. Chastity is sexual purity, but it has various nuances of meaning. It can refer to sexual self-control or moderation, to virginity, to sexual abstinence in Holy Orders, and to sexual continence in marriage. It is one of the three vows taken by monastics (***monk***) and mendicants (***frere***). In general, it is the moral virtue that regulates the sexual appetite in body, mind, and spirit (Matt. 15:17-20; Mark 7:14-23).

From the early Church Fathers, celibacy, total abstinence from sex, was seen as preferable even to lawful sex in marriage. Although there is no biblical injunction to celibacy, from Ambrose to Aquinas and beyond, the Church, following the counsels in the Gospels and the assertions of St. Paul

(1 Cor. 7: 7-8), taught that virginity was a higher state than marriage. Clerical celibacy was practiced from about the fourth century though it was not completely uniform as late as the eleventh century when some exceptions were still made for rural clergy. It was always a part of the commitment of those who lived according to a monastic or friarly rule. Despite fourteenth-century satire about profligate clergy, clerical sexual liaisons were probably not common and certainly not condoned by the Church. (See ***vertu***.)

chaunterie. The chanting or singing of Masses or an endowment for the singing of Masses, usually for the founder. Its meaning extended to a priest or group of priests engaged in such activities, devoted to a life of prayer. More specifically, it came to mean a chantry chapel for donors or supporting families or guilds. Such chapels could be incorporated into a church or be a free-standing structure. Chantry chapels were increasingly popular establishments from the thirteenth century.

cherche, chirche. Any building consecrated for worship, particularly the Eucharistic service. A cathedral was the principal church of a diocese. A collegiate church, often but not necessarily associated with an educational institution, was a place or worship for members of a clerical group.

In a broader sense, the Church was the hierarchical, institutional entity of Christianity or the entire community of Christians united in common belief and worship, sometimes divided into the Church Militant (Christians on earth striving for salvation) and the Church Triumphant (the saved).

chieftaynes of synne. The seven deadly, or capital, sins: pride, greed, lust, anger, gluttony, envy, and sloth. They are both sins in themselves and the underlying dispositions which lead to all other sins. (See ***deedly synnes***.)

(De) Civitate. St. Augustine's *City of God* (*De Civitate Dei*, 413-427), which is distinguished from "civitas terrena", the world of pagans, heretics, and all things secular. ***St. Augustine*** defends the Church, very much a community of faith, from charges of undermining the pagan political authority, and foresees the ultimate triumph of the spiritual in the City of God. Augustine emphasizes the importance, indeed necessity, of the fact of ***Redemption*** for the creation of the City of God. Although the City of God is a spiritual reality, types of it were often seen in terrestrial cities such as Jerusalem and even ***Canterbury***.

Clare, Seint. St. Clare or St. Clere (1194-1253), inspired by St. Francis of Assisi, gave up wealth and founded the Order of Poor Ladies—the Second Order of St. Francis or "Poor Clares". Installed by St. Francis, Clare was abbess at San Damiano from 1215 until her death. Although living according to a modified Benedictine ***rule***, the Poor Clares stressed and embodied poverty and prayer.

clerc, clerk. Medieval usage encompassed members of the clergy, clerics in minor orders, students, scholars, and authors. In its original and strictly ecclesiastical applications, it referred to members of minor orders who were awaiting a benefice before receiving major orders and to a mostly itinerant group of clergy who for one reason or another did not take major orders. Although well educated (most university students could claim to be members of the clergy), they were discouraged from taking secular employment and often forced to live by their wits. From the twelfth century many were employed by the privileged and powerful because of their literacy and intelligence. Their awkward and ambiguous place in society provided opportunities for the acquisition of wealth and temptations to knavery and self-aggrandizement. Rightly or wrongly, their reputation as tricksters and reprobates was highlighted by the Goliardic poets. In fourteenth-century England their reputation ranged from that of scholar to rogue.

cloisterer, cloysterer. A ***monk*** or cloistered nun (***nonne***).

cloistre, cloystre. A large square or rectangular courtyard reserved for the use of ***monks*** in a monastery or nuns (***nonne***) in a convent. It was a place of separation for the monks, devoted to prayer and reading (and washing.) Cloisters probably originated in the eighth century as part of the development of communal monasticism. The intention was to segregate monks from the laity and from all secular distractions. Cloisterer became synonymous with ***monk***. Cloister also applied to the rule of enclosure or separation, which forbade monks and nuns from leaving the enclosure, and sometimes to the monastery as a whole.

(De) Coitu. A treatise on sex by Constantinus Africanus (1015-1087). Primarily a medical rather than a religious work, it was popularly known in the Middle Ages for its information about aphrodisiacs.

complyn. The last of the liturgical hours of the day, from the Latin for "complement" or "completion". This term for the service was first used in the Rule of St. Benedict (***Benedight***), although the practice may have existed previously in the East, and it certainly has spread to the whole Church. In the fourteenth century Compline consisted of psalms (*chanted* at monasteries,) the confession of faults, and a benediction. (See ***monk***.)

confessio(u)n. In its broadest sense confession was a profession of orthodox faith in public attestation, in writing, or in the recitation of an authorized prayer like the ***Confiteor***. More commonly, however, it referred to the ***sacrament*** of ***Penance***. The sacrament required contrition, or sorrow for sin, confession to a priest, a purpose to amend one's life, and satisfaction, by prayer or good works for sins committed. The whole sacrament was generally known as confession because of the practice of auricular confession, private and privileged recitation of one's sins to a priest for the purpose of receiving ***absolution***.

Auricular confession, long controversial in the Church because of the possibility of giving scandal, was deemed necessary by Aquinas for the forgiveness of sins committed after Baptism (***Baptesme***). Confession, however, does not seem to have been frequent in the fourteenth century—several times, at least once, a year appears to have been the norm.

Confiteor. The prayer, a profession of faith, named from its opening word "I confess", *i.e.*, believe. It had the force of a general confession of sins. It was probably composed, pretty much in its modern form, in the tenth century, and by the eleventh century had become part of the public ritual of the Mass (***messe***).

co(u)nseil(e), consielle, councel, counsel(l), counseyl(e), counceil. Advice, particularly on how to lead a perfect Christian life as in "counsels of perfection", which were not precepts or commandments but exhortations to higher spiritual aspiration such as the Beatitudes (Matt. 5:3-10).

A "council", a gathering of ecclesiastics of many types—from ***bishops*** in convocation with the ***Pope***, through priests in conjunction with the bishop of a diocese, to official meetings of a group of monasteries, to a gathering of members of a friary. Councils provided opportunities for discussion and usually issued in conclusions or directions concerning doctrine or policy.

Consolacione. *The Consolation of Philosophy* (c. 524) was the most influential work of Boethius (***Boece***). It is a Platonic dialogue between Boethius and Lady Philosophy, in which she attempts to reconcile him with his imprisonment. Its primary philosophical counsel is to understand the vicissitudes of human life in terms of a higher order. Consequently, the *Consolation* was frequently cited in the controversies over the operations of ***fortune***, ***fate***, free will (***fredom***), and God's foreknowledge (***forknowynge***). Notable authors, including Dante and Jean de Mean noted the need for a translation into the vernacular. Chaucer produced a careful translation, alternating poetic sections with prose sections designed to improve accuracy.

Constantyn. Constantinus Africanus (1015-1087) was a medical scholar, who translated and thereby preserved Arabic treatises. His works were studied at the first and famous medical school at Salerno and taken seriously by European scholars into the sixteenth century. Of special note was ***De Coitu***, his treatise on sex.

contricio(u)n. The interior and sincere sorrow for sin, which was required for ***absolution*** in a valid ***confession***. It required a clear recognition of the offense done to God, the evil done, and a solemn purpose of amendment of one's life. It was sometimes called "perfect contrition", because it was motivated by love of God and sorrow for the offense against Him. It was distinguished from "imperfect contrition" (***attricioun***), which was motivated by the dread of punishment or the fear of the loss of everlasting life. An act of perfect contrition provided the possibility of salvation in the event that the sinner died before receiving formal absolution in the sacrament of Penance. Attrition was efficacious only at the time of the reception of the sacrament. (See ***sacrement***.)

contumacie. The obstinate disregard for legitimate authority, particularly a rebelliousness towards religious authority. As such it was an impediment to the reception of the ***sacrament*** of ***Penance***.

cope. A long outer garment most often associated with ***monks***, friars (***frere***), and nuns (***nonne***). It also could denote a long semi-circular cloak, usually made of silk, worn as a liturgical garment by the ***Pope*** or other prelates (***prelaat***) on ceremonial occasions or the vestment worn by priests (***prest***) for benedictions, vespers, and other prescribed services.

Cordyleres. Franciscan friars (***frere***), whose habit included a rope or belt (or cord) as a cincture around the waist.

Corpus. The Latin word for "body" generally referred to the body of Christ. It is frequently used in mild oaths such as "corpus dominus", "Goddes corpus", and "corpus bones". The most curious usage is "corpus Madrian", used as if Madrian were a saint, though no satisfactory identification of a St. Madrian has been made.

corseynt. A shrine containing the relic (***relike***) of a saint (***seint***); etymologically, the body or a part of the body of the saint. By extension, a shrine even without the presence of a relic or a religious convent devoted to a saint.

COURT CRISTIEN. The ecclesiastical court, which had jurisdiction over crimes committed by members of the clergy and over certain other offenses, committed by laymen but with respect to the Church, ranging from deviations from orthodox belief through public sinfulness like adultery to the failure to pay tithes. These courts often were a source of corruption especially through the devious behavior of their messengers—summoners (***sumnour***). Their powers and abuses provide a particularly vivid insight into the real world of Christianity in Chaucer's time.

The jurisdiction of the ecclesiastical courts initially extended, in a rather restricted way, to Church matters such as property claimed by the Church or clergy, the distribution of benefices, charges of heresy, the payment of tithes, the enforcement of oaths and vows, and episcopal quarrels over diocesan boundaries. Eventually their scope extended to all criminal charges leveled against members of the clergy. The Emperor Constantine decreed that ecclesiastical jurisdiction could obtain whenever the litigants preferred and that the judgments of the ecclesiastical courts would be enforced by the civil authority.

What had begun as gatherings of the faithful in order to sort out spiritual questions under the guidance of legitimate religious authorities developed into a bureaucracy that overlapped and contended with the judicial system of the secular polity. Informal convocations gave way to synodal hearings presided over by the bishop. Eventually even these hearings developed into a tripartite structure as the caseload became too onerous and the issues became more complex. Thus, there emerged the ordinary or archdiaconal courts, which were presided over by archdeacons who were assigned by the bishop to various geographical sub-divisions of the diocese. Archdeacons (***erchedeken***) were minor officials who originally acted as general administrative assistants to the bishops. Presiding over these courts of first resort was added to their other duties, though it eventually occupied most of their time and attention. They did not need to be, and usually were not, members of the clergy, although clerical incumbency became more common as the office became more influential.

Punishments were dealt out by the archdeacon's court for violations of divine law, Church law, and sometimes civil law. The most common issues had to do with the holding or bequeathing of property, marriage, and the payment of tithes. But beyond probate and marriage, the archdeacon's court frequently, especially from the twelfth through the fourteenth century, prosecuted public violations of the moral law such as extortion and concubinage. The punishments that could be meted out included excommunication (the separation of the convicted from the Church, the sacraments, and all contact with the Christian community) and interdict (a similar separation which could be applied to parishes or larger administrative units so that Mass could not be said or the sacraments administered until the conditions of the court had been met). In extreme cases, physical punishment, up to and including death, was possible, though the vast majority of sentences were limited to fines to be paid to the diocese through the court. In day-to-day affairs, the archdeacons became increasingly independent of the bishops they served.

Conflicts between ecclesiastical and civil authorities became more contentious by the end of the twelfth century. For ordinary people in the thirteenth and fourteenth centuries, however, the problems with the ecclesiastical courts and their effects on the lives of the laity were frightening because of the arbitrary, sometimes capricious, power wielded by the archdeacons and their minions, such as summoners. Although court records are not available, there is adequate testimony to the vulnerability felt by much of the ordinary Christian community. Popular and satiric poetry abound with criticism and ridicule of abuses. In some cases, the situation had become almost comical and certainly trivialized. In 1376 the Bishop of Durham threatened excommunication of persons who had stolen a valuable hawk and in 1377 John of Gaunt had the bishops excommunicate *unknown* persons who had vigorously satirized him. On the level of the archdeacon's court the abuses may have been less weighty, but more extensive with regard to all manner of non-tithers and petty thieves—and persons falsely accused of such misdemeanors. The Constitutions of Salisbury (1256) and Boniface, Archbishop of Canterbury, late in the thirteenth century had condemned irregularities, but abuses persisted.

The archdeacon's curse, the formal pronouncement of excommunication, would have been hauntingly familiar to fourteenth century communicants, since it was read, in one form or another, from the pulpit four times a year for admonitory purposes. For most people, the archdeacon's curse, or even the threat of it, was no laughing matter. The number of potential accusations was large and sometimes ambiguous, including slander, arson, treachery, witchcraft, and even contact with an excommunicated person. And the requirements of evidence for making a charge were not high. Especially for the poor, non-payment of tithes was a particular problem since frequently, out of economic necessity, they were in fact guilty. Moreover, the punishments, although extremes were threatened, most often came to fines—oppressive for the poor and lucrative for archdeacons, summoners, and other minor officials. The temptations to and opportunities for abuse were legion. The accused/convicted ordinarily had forty days to pay up to the archdeacon (or bribe the summoner) under pain of a writ of "Significat", which enforced imprisonment until payment was made. No wonder that Chaucer's pilgrim summoner should acknowledge that "purs is the ercedekenes hell" (I, 658). Chaucer's contemporaries, Langland and Gower, agreed.

The pivotal figure in these opportunities for abuse was the summoner. Often paid on the basis of a percentage of fines collected, and out on the front lines relatively free from direct supervision even if the archdeacon cared to supervise, the summoner had enormous opportunities to coerce collections and to extort money from those desperate to avoid indictment by the higher authorities. As G.R. Owst has pointed out (*Literature and Pulpit in Medieval England*), summoners were condemned for abuses by the Council of London (1342) and by parliamentary plea (1378) and it was broadly accepted that "...it is open extorcion, or robbynge. Sumpnours and bedelles, that beth mynistres to the lawe ... robbeth the peple." (MS Harl. 45, fol. 67B) The power of summoners, despite the fact that the definition of their canonical authority never became clear, increased gradually over the thirteenth and fourteenth centuries as they extended, on their own or with the support of the archdeacon, their remit beyond issuing summonses to *de facto* criminal investigation. The practical consequences were that it was frequently in the interest of the summoners to "discover" transgressions and threaten punishment as a means to extort money or, at least by Chaucer's account, sexual and other favors from the trivial to the grievous; the pilgrim summoner would overlook the keeping of a concubine for a year for a quart of wine (I, 649-51).

The fictional summoner in the "Friar's Tale" is well exemplified in the villainies of the pilgrim summoner, who candidly professes to live well by means of systematic abuse of his office. It is interesting that the pilgrim summoner is, with the Pardoner, one of the only two characters for whom even the generous narrator of the General Prologue can find no sympathy—and his physical appearance is even correspondingly disgusting. The corruption of summoners is aptly characterized in the Friar's attack in his Tale (III, 1321-74): in making his daily rounds, the Friar's summoner gathers information, develops a network of informers, including those accused, and even forges documents for evidence. The fact that he attempts to prey on a widow is a sign of his particular power over the lower classes. Yet, even in this satiric portrait it is clear that there is, in the background, an archdeacon who is himself corrupt. There has been much discussion about whether Chaucer's pilgrim summoner was drawn from life. Regardless, it seems likely that both the pilgrim and the Friar's summoner were familiar figures, who represented a corrupt system in which the implementation of ecclesiastical justice had gone out of control—a perception shared by orthodox Catholic Christians and Wyclifites alike. In the popular view, the courts and their representatives were a menace. On a more scholarly level, John Bromyard, a Dominican preacher around the turn of the fifteenth century, made clear in his *Summa Praedicantium*, a rather sophisticated handbook for preachers, that many intellectuals saw the summoners, archdeacons, and even the bishops themselves to be enmeshed in a tangle of corruption.

FURTHER READING: G.R. Owst, *Literature and Pulpit in Medieval England* (Cambridge: Cambridge University Press, 1933); Robert E. Rodes, *Ecclesiastical Administration in Medieval England* (Notre Dame: Notre Dame University Press, 1977); Richard M. Wunderli, *London Church Courts and Society on the Eve of the Reformation* (Cambridge, MA: Medieval Academy of America, 1981).

covent. A religious establishment of either sex (monks, friars, canons, nuns) living together under one ***rule***, roughly equivalent to "monastery". The word also applied to the structure in which they lived. Sometimes spelled "convent", though not by Chaucer, the word was derived from the assemblies of Roman citizens in provinces. (See ***monk***.)

cove(i)tise, coveityse, coveytise, coveytyse. One of the seven deadly sins (***deedly synnes***) and thus more important as a disposition than a specific act. Although it is broadly synonymous with greed or avarice (q.v.), Chaucer's Parson makes the distinction that avarice is a generalized inappropriate desire for what we do not have, covetousness is a desire for what rightly belongs to another.

C(H)RIST. Jesus Christ, the second person of the Blessed Trinity (***trinitee***), whose suffering and death redeemed man from the original sin of Adam and was validated by his Resurrection from the dead, the prime event of the Christian revelation. Forms of his name are often used in oaths, bordering on blasphemy (***blasphemynge***), though such invocations of the Redeemer are more often made by using the more indirect word "corpus". The frequency of the invocation of Christ, seriously or casually, by whatever title, is rather a sign of the immediacy of the Christian revelation than of disrespect.

Indeed, orthodox theology often found lively expression in daily life and popular devotion, however dubious were some customs and practices. Two practices deserve particular attention: pilgrimages and passion plays. ***Pilgrimages*** are journeys to sacred places. For Medieval Europe the most important places were those where Jesus lived and died in and around Jerusalem. Pious pilgrims sought to imitate Christ in their own lives, to die and rise with him by "dying to sin" and "rising to eternal life"; symbolically, to go up to Jerusalem, the Holy City, was to go to heaven. Pilgrims returning from this "Holy Land" inspired those unable to make the actual pilgrimage to dramatize in their own locales the events in the life of Christ by the so-called "passion plays". Although the term "***passion***" here refers most properly to the suffering and death of Jesus, the subject matter of passion plays included events throughout his life. By the fifteenth century these passion plays, and the events that they dramatized, were called "mysteries" (from the Latin *ministerium*, meaning "act" or "drama"). Meditations on these mysteries were eventually grouped chronologically into three sets: the joyful, the sorrowful, and the glorious, corresponding not only to the sequence of events in Christ's life but also to the typical stages in the life of every Christian. Thus, both pilgrimages and passion plays in a parallel way dramatized both Christ's life and, figuratively, human lives.

Thus, the life of Jesus begins joyfully with these events: the Annunciation (Luke 1:26-38), the Visitation (Luke 1:40-55), the Birth (Luke 2:6-20), the Epiphany (Matt. 2:1-12), the Circumcision and Presentation (Luke 2:21-39), the Flight into Egypt and the Slaughter of the

Innocents (Matt. 2:13-18), and the Finding in the Temple (Luke 2:41-51). In these episodes, the doctrine of the Incarnation is vividly conveyed: Jesus is the eternal Word of God who becomes fully human without losing his divinity and fulfills all the promises God made to the Israelites; he is the long-awaited Anointed One (*Christos* in Greek) with a triple role: Priest, Prophet, and Ruler. Through the Incarnation, Jesus, the Son of God, reveals most fully Who God is and how much he loves us. Through his Incarnation, he saves us, sanctifies us, and shares his divine life with us.

Later church councils stated in precise philosophical terms that Jesus is one divine person with two distinct natures (divine and human). Such philosophical precision was required by the perennial tendency to oversimplify the articles of Christian faith and the failure to make necessary distinctions. In general, the major Christological heresies can be understood as attempts to make sense of Christ's divinity at the expense of his humanity or, vice versa, to make sense of his humanity at the expense of his divinity. Thus, for example, Gnostic Docetism claimed that the divine Christ merely took on the appearance of a man but not real humanity. Adoptionism, on the other hand, allowed that Jesus was divinized by a kind of "adoption" by God but denied that he was God by nature; Arianism claimed that Christ was the most exalted of creatures, but a creature nonetheless, not God. Alternatively, Nestorianism held that Christ was a human person joined to a divine person (the Son of God) but that these two persons were so distinct that Mary was only the mother of Jesus, not the mother of God. Then Monophysitism restored belief in the unity of the divine person, the Son of God, by claiming that Christ's human nature ceased to be human once it was united to God; similarly, Apollinarianism held that Christ's divinity took the place of a human soul. In each case, orthodox Christianity steered a middle course between these opposing simplifications and insisted that Christ is both fully divine and fully human, and fully unified as a single person.

Sorrowful mysteries in the life of Jesus are the Agony in the Garden (Matt. 26:36-46), the Scourging at the Pillar (Matt. 27:26), the Crowning with Thorns (Matt. 27:29), the Carrying of the Cross (Luke 23:26-32), the Crucifixion (Luke 23:33-46), and the Descent into hell (1 Peter 3:19-20; 4:6)—as he descends into hell, he preaches to the righteous souls imprisoned there, and thus "harrows" hell by redeeming these souls. ("The Harrowing of Hell" is one of the oldest extant English passion plays, dating from the thirteenth century.) In these episodes, the doctrine of the Atonement or ***Redemption*** is portrayed. Literally, redemption is a "buying back", the payment of a ransom. In this case, a sinless man offers himself in sacrifice as an innocent victim of cruelty and injustice. Through the merits of his suffering and death, he wins forgiveness for the sins of the world, rescues mankind from the bondage of sin incurred by the Fall of Adam, and reconciles humanity to God. Because Adam's sin was an offense against the infinite God, only the infinite merits of Christ's Passion and Crucifixion could provide condign ransom or satisfaction. Since he is divine as well as human, his offering on behalf of all humanity is of infinite worth, an inexhaustible treasury of grace. Christ's redemption of mankind is the central fact of Christianity, the event which makes possible human ***salvation***, and the very purpose of the Incarnation.

Christ's life does not end with his death, however, nor does the life of the Christian. Rather, life culminates in the glorious mysteries: Resurrection (Luke 24:1-12), Ascension (Luke 24:50-51), Pentecost (Acts 2:1-4), Assumption (1 Thess. 4:16-17) and Coronation (Rev. 12:1; 21:1-22:5), and Last Judgment (Matt. 25:31-46). In the Resurrection, he is fully restored, with a glorified body no longer bound by space and time, so that he may appear to his disciples how and when he will. In these appearances, he shows that God the Father has accepted his saving sacrifice and that he has conquered death for all mankind. Though glorified, this body ("corpus") is tangible as well as visible (John 20:26-29), and in his risen glory, Jesus eats with his disciples (Luke 24:30, 36-43; John 21:9-14). Moreover, as Medieval Christians vividly believed, in his risen body, now no longer visible but present under the sacramental appearances of bread and wine, he is simultaneously present, whole and entire, throughout the world wherever Mass (***messe***) is celebrated or the Blessed Sacrament is reserved.

As a sign of the church's destiny, Jesus takes his mother Mary, body and soul, to heaven at the end of her life (Assumption) and crowns her with glory (Coronation). So, too, the church, with all her faithful members, will rise with glorified bodies to live with Christ forever in heaven. This is ultimately the destination of all pious pilgrimages, wherever their destinations may be on earth. Heaven (***salvation***) is the achievement or condition of everlasting glory and life with God, enjoying the Beatific Vision—the immediate perception of God. It is, finally, a gift of God's grace, even though it is achieved in a life of good works and charity. As the final goal of all Christians, it gives meaning to human existence. The opposite of salvation is ***damnation***: eternal separation from God. Just as man's ultimate happiness consists in eternal life with God, his ultimate misery (***helle***) is eternal separation from God. At the end of each man's life, he will be judged individually by God (the Particular Judgment), with Purgatory a possibility; at the Second Coming at the end of time, everyone will be judged by Christ (the General or Last Judgment—Matt. 25:31-46), to be punished forever in hell or rewarded forever in heaven. Those who die in the state of grace are saved; those who die in mortal (serious or grave) sin are damned. Since only what is holy can enter God's presence, those who die in the state of grace but hampered by the temporal effects of sin (*e.g.*, spiritual sluggishness or inordinate attachments to creatures) are purified of these effects through a transient condition called ***purgatorie***.

These so-called "Four Last Things"—death, judgment, heaven, and hell—were stock themes in Medieval preaching, passion plays, pilgrimages, and piety: God wills the salvation of all; man damns himself by sin; Christ opens the gates of heaven once again; man, united to Christ by acts of faith, works of love, and celebration of the sacraments, makes his pilgrimage to heaven via purgation either here or hereafter.

Liturgically, the year itself took the shape of an annual pilgrimage through the life, death, and resurrection of Jesus: beginning with Advent in the late fall, after the harvest, as the natural world lies dormant; centering on the spring celebration of the birth of the new life; and finally, progressing thence to the final "harvest" at the end of time. The annual cycles of nature themselves reflected the mysteries: after death enters the world by the sin of Adam, the world awaits the "advent" of its savior, who comes just as the world is darkest (the winter solstice). As the days gradually lengthen, and the dryness is moistened by sweet spring rains, the light of the world shines forth in the life and teaching of Jesus. ("Than longen folk to goon on pilgrimages.") As light and darkness are poised in equal measure (the spring equinox), life and death are locked in mortal combat on the Cross. But life and light win out over darkness and death: Jesus rises from the dead, ascends into heaven, sends his Holy Spirit on the Church (Pentecost), like the sun in a summer sky. In the time after Pentecost, the Church, while laboring in the fields and vineyards to prepare a rich harvest, awaits the return of her Lord at the end of time.

In all these mysteries the doctrine of the Trinity (***trinitee***), the core doctrine of Christianity, is exemplified: one God, with a single divine nature, in three divine persons—the Father, the Son, and the Holy Spirit, such that the Father is not the Son, the Son is not the Holy Spirit, the Holy Spirit is not the Father, but the Father is God, the Son is God, and the Holy Spirit is God, the one and only God. In the eternal Now beyond all time the Father lovingly generates the Son, the Son lovingly receives the self-donation of the Father, and the very love between Father and Son is love personified, the Holy Spirit. All the universe of creatures originates in this gratuitous outpouring of eternal love. All history moves towards this love as its ultimate goal. Jesus, the Incarnate Word of the Father, is the center of history, recapitulating all nature, all human events, all loves in his life, death, and resurrection.

As with the Incarnation, the doctrine of the Trinity developed with greater precision by confronting heretical tendencies to oversimplification.

In addition to the Christological heresies mentioned above, which were also heresies about the Trinity, Sabellianism claimed that the three persons of the Trinity were merely modes or manifestations of the one God—that the threeness was only apparent but not real. Orthodox Christianity, however, insisted on the real plurality of persons within the utter unity of God. It is in the mutual self-giving of these persons that the deepest nature of God is revealed as a community of love; the eternal and perfect love of Christ for God the Father takes human form in the Incarnation. By Christ's death and resurrection, that same love is extended to all humankind in the Redemption. By the grace Christ won for us, we in turn can extend that love to others and thus fulfill the deepest human desire to love and to be loved, by sharing in the very life of the Trinity, imperfectly on earth but perfectly in heaven. The unconsummated longing of the troubadours of courtly love thus found its most profound Medieval rejoinder in the life, death, and glorification of Christ.

FURTHER READING: Karl Adam, *The Christ of Faith: The Christology of the Church*, tr. Joyce Crick (New York: New American Library, 1962); Gerald O'Collins, *Christology: A Biblical, Historical, and Systematic Study of Jesus* (New York: Oxford University Press, 1996); Thomas Langan, *The Catholic Tradition*, Ch. 7: "Medieval Catholicism: Living an Incarnational Religion", pp. 176-202 (Columbus, MO: University of Missouri Press, 1998); Marilyn McCord Adams, *What Sort of Human Nature: Medieval Philosophy and the Systematics of Christology* (Milwaukee: Marquette University Press, 1999).

Cristen(e), Cristien. A Christian; a baptized member of the Christian Church.

Cristendom. Although the term can refer to the Christian faith or to the Church, its more common use is for the lands and peoples encompassed by the Christian faith as compared to the heathen, non-Christian world (***hethenesse***).

Cristenmasse. The day on which the birth of Christ is celebrated. Although the specific date was disputed in the early Church, December 25 had long been settled upon by the fourteenth century. Preceded by the anticipatory liturgical season of Advent, Christmas was celebrated for the birth of the Redeemer (***redempcioun***) as a feast second only to Easter.

cristned. Baptized, *i.e.*, having received the ***sacrament*** of Baptism (***Baptesme***). Baptism removed, or cleansed, the original sin imputed to all human beings from the sin of Adam and Eve and formally received persons into the Christian community. In the early Church, Baptism could only be received after a long period of instruction and trial, but, by the fourteenth century, infant Baptism had become customary for the children of Christian parents.

Cristyanytee. The Christian religion.

croce, cros(s), crois, croys. Variants of the word cross referring, most specifically, to the cross on which Christ was crucified and which has become a conventional symbol of Christianity because of its association with the sacrifice of Christ, the quintessential act of ***Redemption***. In the early Middle Ages the cross as an artifact did not include the body of Christ, but gradually this became more common and the crucifix, strictly speaking, developed.

culpe. Fault or guilt, especially the guilt of sin. The negative effects of sin are two-fold: guilt ("culpe") and punishment ("***payne***"). Guilt is personal blameworthiness for wrongdoing, whereas punishment or atonement may be completed by an innocent person in place of the guilty one. Thus, the sinless Jesus' suffering and death, as punishment for original sin, takes away the guilt of those who repent and believe in Him. By Christ's merits, one's guilt may be forgiven—by Baptism (***Baptesme***) or ***Penance***, for instance—even before temporal (purgatorial) punishment is entirely completed. (See ***Crist***, ***Purgatorie***.)

cura(a)t. A parish priest, that is a clergyman who has entrusted to him a geographical jurisdiction, based in a church, for serving the spiritual needs of the surrounding community by saying Mass, administering the sacraments, and generally attending to the spiritual welfare of his parishioners. A curate was synonymous with ***parson*** although it later came to be applied to the assistant to the pastor of a parish. Earlier on the curate had the spiritual responsibility and his assistants were called "vicars" (***vicaire***). The reputation of curates and parsons was relatively good in the fourteenth century, because of their often devoted service during the plague of 1348 and their relative poverty. Not so with the members of religious orders and prelates, who were often viewed as corrupted by greed and self-indulgence.

cure. Although there are general meanings of attention to, responsibility for, and regard for, the religious sense has to do with the cure (care) of souls, which spiritual responsibility was that of the ***curate*** or ***parson*** within the jurisdiction of the parish, but more broadly the responsibility of all the clergy. It could refer to the physical jurisdiction itself, such as the parish of a curate or the diocese of a ***bishop***.

curs(e). In the most general sense, a curse was ***damnation***, (*i.e.*, Christes curs). In common parlance, however, the more common application was to excommunication, a judgment on an individual excluding him from Mass, the sacraments, and participation in all communal rituals. The effect was to cut off the individual from participation in the Christian community, indeed from salvation, barring recantation, contrition, and public penance. Although the "curs" could be imposed by a priest, it was more often done by the bishop or the bishop's archdeacon (***erchedeken***), who presided over the ecclesiastical court (***Court Cristien***). Thus the fear of the "archdeacon's curse", (***ercedecenes curs***). On a broader scale a "curs" could be an interdict, a ruling by the Pope or bishop as a punishment on a parish or other jurisdiction forbidding the performance of all spiritual rites until repentant reconciliation with ecclesiastical authority was effected.

Cutberd, Seint. St. Cuthbert (c. 635-687) was an English monk and patron of Durham. He became prior at the famous monastery at Lindisfarne in order to introduce reforms dictated by the Synod of Whitby (664), which attempted to restrain Celtic deviations from Roman practice. Eventually he became bishop of Lindisfarne, and many miracles were attributed to him within a short period after his death.

Dalida, Dalyda. Samson, the Biblical Jewish champion, fell in love with Delilah (Judges 16), who was probably a Philistine prostitute. The Philistine princes bribed her to find out the source of Samson's legendary strength. On her fourth attempt she got Samson to admit that it was his uncut hair, a sign of his commitment to the Nazarites. They then cut off his hair and delivered him, blinded, to Gaza. Delilah is the very type of the perfidious woman and, in the anti-feminist tradition, she is often listed in the catalogues of temptresses along with Eve.

Damasie, Seint. St. Damasus (c. 304-384) was a Roman who was elected Pope overwhelmingly in 366, though his election was afterwards disputed unsuccessfully. He is the probable founder of the Vatican Archives. St. Jerome (***Jeremie***) reports that Damasus wrote on virginity, but the text or texts are not extant.

dampnacioun, dampnyng. The condemnation to eternal punishment in ***hell*** of an individual who dies in a state of unforgiven serious sin. The pains of the damned are twofold: 1. Poena sensus, the sensory pain, according to long tradition, of fire; 2. Poena damni, the pain of loss, which arises from the realization of the damned soul that he or she will never experience the "Beatific Vision", the direct experience of God, the end and purpose of our being.

Consignment to hell is made immediately after death (Particular Judgment) and again at the Second Coming of Christ, the end of the world (General Judgment). Damnation was seen as a manifestation of divine justice and the Last Judgment was seen as an appropriate public manifestation so that God's justice would be seen ultimately to prevail.

Although the pain of loss was consistently held to be greater than the pain of fire, popular preachers emphasized the latter in a tradition of horrific oratory urging the faithful to repent and reform. In a world immersed in sincere belief and surrounded by constant reminders of death, the terrors of damnation were an effective motivation to virtue.

Daniel, Danyel. Daniel was a Jewish hero and the traditional author of the prophetic Book of Daniel. Of the tribe of Judah, he was captured and taken to Babylon by Nebuchadnezzar (***Nabugodonosor***) where he was educated in the mysteries of the Chaldeans and became a court favorite, with his three companions Sidrach, Misach, and Abdenago. He increased his fame and favor by interpreting Nebuchadnezzar's dreams when the court wise men were stymied. This is especially true of Nebuchadnezzar's second dream in which he is told to cut down a tree but leave the stump standing. Daniel interpreted that the king would be punished for pride but that the kingdom would be restored.

Later, at a drunken feast fueled by wine stolen from the temple in Jerusalem, a disembodied hand writes "Mene, Thecel, Phares" on the wall, and Daniel is the only one able to interpret the destructive warning of the "handwriting on the wall". Once again privileged, Daniel was caught praying during a period when all petitions, except to the monarch Darius, were forbidden. He was put in the lion's den but was miraculously preserved.

Daniel was a prophet of punishment and desolation to come on the Gentiles and, in the second half of his Book, foretells the coming of the Messianic kingdom, an optimistic prophesy for the Jews and a prediction of Christ for Christians. (See ***scripture***.)

David, Davit. David was anointed as the second king of Israel, succeeding Saul because of Saul's disobedience (1 Sam. – 1 Kings 2:10). Renowned as a musician, he was sent to sing to soothe Saul during his war against the Philistines. His most impressive, and memorable, victory was his defeat of the giant Goliath, which became a symbol of the triumph of the virtues. David was a warrior-king, who made Israel an independent state, conquered Jerusalem ("the city of David"), and brought the Ark of the Covenant there. After falling into murder (of Urias) and an adulterous affair with Bathsheba, he became a model of penitents. His Messianic prophecies are contained in the Psalms. (See ***scripture***.)

decree. Any statement of law or policy, but used especially with regard to official pronouncements or public interpretations of divine or canon law.

Decrees (Book of). The *Decretals of Gratian, Corpus juris canonice* (c. 1150), familiarly called the *Decretum of Gratian*, was considered a code of ecclesiastical laws. Decretals are pontifical decisions communicated in a letter. They are not necessarily general or universal laws of the Church, but responses to questions or clarifications of matters of "discipline" rather than dogma. Gratian's book was a compilation of Papal decrees, achieved a degree of authority, and was widely commented upon in the succeeding centuries. Thus, Gratian, a scholarly monk, became known as the founder of canon law.

deedly (synnes). Deadly sins are the dispositions that underlie all other sins. Sin is "the willing of a changeable good in an inordinate way, so that it involves a turning away from the unchangeable God", according to St. Thomas Aquinas (ST.I-II.84.1). St. Gregory the Great (540?-604) refers to seven sins as "capital" sins because they lead to other sins. A deadly sin could also mean any serious, or mortal, sin—one which brings death to the soul and bars salvation unless confessed and absolved in the sacrament of *Penance*. Also called "the seven capital sins" because they are fundamental moral failings that give rise to many other faults. In Dante's *Purgatorio* (Canto XVII), Virgil explains to pilgrim Dante how love is at the root of these seven vices: love may either be misdirected or rightly directed. It is misdirected in three ways: pride, envy, and anger, all of which make harm to one's neighbor a perverse object of love. Even when it is rightly directed, love may be faulty by excess or deficiency. Love deficient is sloth; love excessive takes the form of avarice, gluttony, and lust. Thus, the seven deadly sins are pride, envy, anger, sloth, avarice, gluttony, and lust (also called "luxury"). They were frequently used as a means (a kind of "checklist") for the examination of conscience before auricular ("in the ear" of a priest) ***Confession***. They are prominent in Chaucer from the concentration of the Pardoner, for his own rhetorical purposes, on gluttony and lust (the so-called "tavern sins") to the Parson's elaborate definitions of each of the seven and his proposals of "remedies" for each as part of his treatise on ***Penitence***.

dekne. Deacons were servants or ministers, based on Acts 6:1-6 where they are directed to serve widows. Tradition has it that St. Stephen was the first deacon. In the early Church their role was to relieve bishops and priests of their more secular preoccupations. They read announcements at Mass and often acted as the bishop's deputy, retaining a special mission to widows and the poor. They also attended to details: by preparing the sacred vessels for Mass, by reading the designated Scriptural passages, and by doing "crowd control" when necessary. Although deacons were not priests, the office evolved into a ritual stepping stone to the priesthood, and the duties of deacons became more specifically ceremonial, *e.g.* distribution of Communion and exposition of the Blessed Sacrament at Benediction.

demonyak. Someone possessed by the devil. Possession is found in many ancient religions, is amply attested in ***Scripture***, and is, indeed the first wonder described in the Gospel of ***St. Mark***. Possession might be a sign of slavery to sin, but not necessarily. Sometimes there are physical manifestations such as blindness, dumbness, or insanity, but it is essentially the entry of an evil spirit, one of the fallen angels, into the host for whatever reason. The casting out of demons by Christ was often accompanied by the disappearance of physical symptoms as well as the less tangible spiritual liberation. Christ's casting out of demons was an impressive sign of His power to His disciples.

Denys, Seint. St. Denis (d. c. 275) was the first bishop of Paris and a martyr. He built a church on the Ile St. Louis and provided regular Christian services. Opposed by the pagan Gaulish priests, he was scourged, put on the rack, confined with wild beasts, imprisoned, and beheaded, although this gruesome account dates from several centuries after his death. He is often pictured with his head in his hands because, after his execution, he is reported to have walked some distance.

In the Middle Ages, St. Denis was often confused with Dionysius the Areopagite, converted by ***St. Paul***, and with the Pseudo-Dionysius, the composer of the Areopagitic writings in the second half of the fifth century.

despeir, disespeyr, dispaire, dispayr, dispeir(e). Despair is often used in secular contexts to mean complete disheartenment or lack of hope. In a spiritual sense it is a loss of confidence in the mercy of God in the face of the magnitude or gravity of our sins, even repented. It is a voluntary and complete abandonment of hope of salvation, one of the three theological virtues. A mistaken conviction that our sins are too great, salvation is too difficult to achieve, or God places limits on His willingness to pardon, despair is a sin which, if persisted in, cannot be forgiven and leads to ***damnation***.

dette. In addition to the ordinary sense of debt, indebtedness, or obligation, dette was commonly used to refer to the marriage or wedding debt—the obligation or responsibility of, especially, the woman in marriage to engage in sexual intercourse. Although the lawfulness of sex even in marriage had long been argued, the mutual obligation to engage in sex required the intention to conceive children. Despite doubts about marital sex and the idea of a wedding "dette", there is no evidence that people in the Middle Ages refrained from full, sometimes energetic, sexual expression.

devel, devil. Primarily Satan (***Sathan***), the leader of the fallen angels in rebellion against God. The devil persistently endeavors to corrupt human beings and deflect them from God and ***salvation***. Especially in the plural, the word can signify lesser demonic spirits or forces who tempt the Christian towards ***damnation***. In contrast to gnostic heresies, orthodox

Christianity regards Satan as vastly superior to man in intelligence but infinitely inferior to God in power. Human life is a battle between sinners seeking salvation and Satan seeking the damnation of all. Satan is destined to lose, but you wouldn't know that by looking around.

devyn(e), dyvyn(e). As an adjective it refers to association with the divinity or with holy or sacred things. As a noun, it indicates a theologian or a very holy person. The "service dyvyne" probably is the Mass (**messe**) but could refer to other liturgical observances.

Dives. The rich man in the parable told by Luke (16: 19-31). The name is not used in the Gospel, but came into vogue (Latin: rich) in the Middle Ages. In life, poor Lazarus, covered with sores, fed from the oblivious Dives' table crumbs. After death Lazarus is received into the bosom of Abraham while Dives suffers the tortures of the damned. Dives calls on God to send Lazarus with water, but he is refused because he had comforts in his terrestrial life. The story is a cautionary tale about the danger of riches, which may cause us to pay too much attention to the world, and an exaltation of poverty as a means to spiritual liberation.

doctour. A learned teacher of orthodox Christian doctrine. The requirements for the designation are distinguished interpretation of doctrine, a holy life, and declaration by the Church, though this declaration does not seem to have been necessarily Papal. In the early Middle Ages, the only Doctors were the four Latin Fathers (Gregory the Great, Ambrose, Augustine, and Jerome) and the three Eastern Fathers (John Chrysostom, Basil, and Gregory Nazianzen). Later, Medieval scholars, such as Anselm and Aquinas were accorded the title.

doctrine, doctryne. Doctrine is a body of teaching in general, but specifically it is the dogmatic teaching that issues from the "magisterium", the teaching authority of the Church. It consists of those things which must be believed if one is to live the good life, be consistent with the Church, and ultimately achieve ***salvation.*** The fullness of revelation is the person of Christ. In all that he did, suffered, and taught during his earthly life, Jesus was the original source of Christian doctrine. All Christian doctrine worthy of the name, then, must in some sense be traced back to Jesus. All of history and indeed all of creation are sources of Christian doctrine in the extended sense that they are included in the mystery of Christ: Christ is both the Word (*Logos*) through whom the world was created and also the center of history, which leads up to his first coming as man and thence to his final coming as Lord. Just as the acorn draws nutrients from its environment to unfold the plan fully contained within it, so too does Christian doctrine draw from creation and history (for both are divinely governed) to exfoliate the mystery fully contained in the person of Jesus.

A mystery in this sense is not unfathomable obscurity but inexhaustible revelation—we can never get to the bottom of it but we can plumb it ever more deeply. Thus Christian doctrine develops and becomes more explicit over time. Ever more exact doctrinal formulae serve to keep us open to the mystery of Christ when we are tempted to foreclose it by oversimplifying. Such temptations have stimulated deeper theological reflection and doctrinal development. For instance, it seems paradoxical, if not altogether contradictory, to teach that Jesus is completely human and at the same time completely divine. If to be human is to be essentially mortal and to be divine is to be essentially immortal, how can Jesus be both? The rational mind is tempted to emphasize his humanity to the neglect of his divinity, or vice versa. In fact, this has been the pattern of heresies about Jesus down through the centuries—to purchase simplicity and clarity at the expense of orthodoxy and mystery. Thus, for instance, Arians denied Jesus' equality with God. Docetists, on the other hand, denied that Jesus was really human but regarded him as God merely appearing in human guise. Orthodox Christian doctrine has repeatedly rejected heresies on both sides by asserting the humanly incomprehensible mystery of Christ in the formula, "Jesus is one divine person, hypostatically uniting two natures, one fully human, the other fully divine." Christians see divine guidance in such persistent and recalcitrant orthodoxy in the face of the tempting "clarifications" and trendy adaptations of every age. (See ***scripture***, ***heresye***.)

The doctrines of the Trinity (***trinitee***), the Incarnation, and ***Redemption*** are central to Christian faith. The two doctrines of the Incarnation and the Resurrection of the Body flowered in the High Middle Ages in widespread devotion to the bodies, body parts, and bodily accouterments of saints insofar as these were vehicles of holiness. (See ***pilgrimage*** and ***relikes***.)

dom, domesday. The Last Judgment or the day of the Last Judgment when, at the end of the world, ***Christ*** will come to judge "the living and the dead". The term has a secular or legal sense, but its religious application is ubiquitous. Although there is punishment assigned at the time of individual death, there still must be a General Judgment at the Second Coming of

Christ, the parousia, as a public vindication of Divine Providence (*purveaunce*) in the division of the just from the sinful. Copious references to such a public manifestation exist in Scripture and it appears as an article of faith, looked upon with some foreboding, in both the Nicene Creed and the Apostles' Creed.

dortour. A dormitory in a convent or a monastery, it would be a single room austerely furnished.

Dunstan, Seint. St. Dunstan (c. 908-988) was an archbishop, confessor (one who suffered for the faith but was not martyred), and perhaps the greatest of the Anglo-Saxon saints. Devoted to learning and crafts, he suffered humiliation at the hands of enemies jealous of his preferment, who cast him into a cesspool. Although he lived as a hermit at Glastonbury, he was called to public distinction, becoming Archbishop of Canterbury in 978, where he withdrew from public affairs to a simple life despite his episcopacy. He was reputed to have the power to control devils probably because of his cure from a dreadful attack of boils, perhaps brought on by the cesspool. Second only to ***St. Thomas*** a Becket in veneration by the English Church.

ecclesiaste. Sometimes a churchman or member of the clergy. More often the Book of Ecclesiasticus, also known as the Book of Sirach, the longest of the deuterocanonical works, a "wisdom book" full of sage counsel. The first part consists mostly of pronouncements on how the truly wise and God-fearing man will behave. The second part is a history of wisdom in the lives of distinguished Jewish historical figures. (See ***scripture***.)

Edward, Seint. St. Edward the Confessor (1003-1066) was King of England from 1043-1066. He spent his childhood in Normandy studying and doing holy things. During his reign he repealed the Danegeld and avoided other taxation, lived on his own wealth, and presided over a period of peace and prosperity frequently and nostalgically recalled as "the good old days". Although he took a vow of celibacy, he continued to live, though continently, with his wife Edith. The title Confessor indicates that he suffered for his faith, primarily by restraint and self-denial. He was buried at Westminster Abbey (of St. Peter), which he had re-built, and was canonized in 1161 by Pope Alexander III. His body was "translated", that is, moved to a more desirable location, in the presence of ***St. Thomas*** and Henry II on October 13, 1163. His enduring reputation is for personal holiness and almsgiving.

Eleyne, Seint. St. Helena (c. 247-327) was the mother of Constantine the Great and, according to legend, the daughter of an English prince. Her husband, Constantius Chlorus having left her, she was restored to court by her son, became devout, and was instructed in Christianity under his direction. She founded churches in the Holy Land and, about 326 at the unearthing of the Church of the Holy Sepulchre, is reputed to have discovered the "True Cross", the cross on which Christ was crucified. Constantine erected a basilica on the spot.

Part of the Cross was left and the rest sent to Constantine at Constantinople. Because it was believed that as the Cross was cut into pieces it miraculously never got smaller, relics of the True Cross were common in the Middle Ages and over time there must have been enough to have built a medium-sized city.

Eliachim. The high priest, Joachim in the Authorized Version (Judith 4: 6-7), who ordered arming the passes as Holofernes' (***Oloferne***) army approached and prayed, fasted, and covered himself with penitential ashes. He is a symbol of resistance to evil.

Elise. The prophet Elisha, or Eliseus, who was a disciple of and successor to Elijah the miracle worker (2 Kings 2). He assumed the mantle of Elijah upon the latter's "translation" into heaven from the hills of Moab.

Elye. The prophet Elijah (1 Kings 19:8; 2 Kings 2:11). He proclaimed the evil of the age and "proved" the superiority of Jehovah over the pagan god Baal in a contest of sacrifices on Mount Carmel. Subsequently he fled to Mt. Horeb where he fasted and prophesied. Elijah was taken from the hills of Moab ("translated") by a chariot of fire in a whirlwind, and thus did not experience death in any ordinary sense.

Ennok. Scripture (Gen. 5:18-24) intimates that Enoch was taken into heaven without death after 365 years of life. The story of his "translation" into heaven is supported by the apocryphal Book of Henoch and the New Testament Letter to the Hebrews (11:5).

enterdited, entredited. Originally from the French meaning "entry forbidden", it is the past verbal form of interdict, a censure or punishment imposed by the Pope or a bishop for a serious crime. As a punishment interdict differs from excommunication in that it does not separate an individual or group from Christian association or exclude one from the community of the faithful. The most common kinds involve the suspension of a priest, the suspension of worship in a particular church, the prohibition of a particular act of worship or devotional practice. Broadly speaking, it may be applied to a territory or city (the most common form in the Middle Ages), to a group of laymen or clergy, to a specific church, or to a specific bishop or cleric. It prohibits the interdicted place(s) or person(s) from access to all or some of the liturgy or acts of worship, from some or all of the ***sacraments*** except in case of necessity, and/or from Christian burial. Interdict is a temporary punishment. In the case of an individual, it may be removed by receiving ***absolution***. In cases where it falls on a location or a class of people, it is generally lifted after a specified period of time.

Of the two instances of interdict mentioned in Chaucer, one is of a priest and the other is of a church. Thus, the church would be forbidden to be the site of worship and the priest would be forbidden to perform the liturgy.

envie, envye. One of the seven deadly sins (***deedly synnes***), envy is sorrow or regret over the prosperity or well being of another. The Parson, apparently following ***St. Augustine***, deems it a sin against the Holy Ghost because it proceeds from malice (whereas the Holy Ghost proceeds from the everlasting love between the Father and the Son). It is, therefore, a challenge against the very Providence (***purveaunce***) of God, an objection to His Divine plan. The Parson calls it the worst sin, although that place is more usually given to pride.

epistel, epistle. Epistle can be a reference to Ovid's Epistles, but in the religious context of the "Tale of Melibee" it refers to the canonical letters in the Christian ***Scriptures***. These apostolic letters are sometimes named for the author (***St. Paul***, ***St. James***) and sometimes for the addressees (Corinthians, Hebrews). They contain teaching, encouragement, and exhortations to orthodoxy in following the Christian revelation.

ercedeken(es), erchedeken. The ecclesiastical office of archdeacon first appeared in diocesan administration in the fourth century and lasted until the fifteenth. The archdeacon was a special confidant, advisor, lieutenant, and dogsbody of the bishop. He supervised the other deacons (***dekne***) and managed Church property. Because the archdeacon had a traditional responsibility for care of the poor, a grasping or self-serving archdeacon is both uniquely reprehensible and not entirely unheard of. The authority of archdeacons peaked in the eleventh and twelfth centuries and sometimes they acted as deputed guardians of the faith. It was not required that they be clergy, though they often were. Although restraint on their powers began in the thirteenth century, in the Fourteenth they still presided over the ecclesiastical courts (***Court Cristien***) of first instance (the bishop heard appeals) and could punish both clergy and laity with penalties as severe as excommunication.

ercedekenes curs. The archdeacon's curse was excommunication. Although there were many kinds of excommunication enmeshed in a tangle of canon law, essentially it was the most serious penalty the Church could inflict, though its purpose was to correct or reform rather than punish. Excommunication resulted in the deprivation of an individual of all Christian rights. The practice is founded on the notion that the Church is a society and therefore has the right to exclude members (baptized Christians, not Jews or pagans who are by definition not members) from participation. Intended to apply only to the most serious infractions, excommunication excluded a person from the reception of the sacraments, from participation in public rituals and prayers, from receiving indulgences (***pardoun***), from Christian burial, indeed from all the perquisites of membership in the Christian community including social intercourse with the rest of the faithful. Practical exceptions were made for the performance of obligations required by civil law or domestic responsibilities.

Excommunication had been practiced from the time of the early Church. Historically, it was a penalty reserved for imposition by the ***Pope***, ***bishops***, religious superiors, and other prelates (***prelat***), and not permitted to parish priests. Release from excommunication was ordinarily reserved to the ecclesiastical authority who had originally imposed it, though exceptions were made for persons in danger of death. Excommunication proliferated in the fourteenth century, resulting in the extension of the right to minor officials such as archdeacons, by whom it was frequently abused for authoritarian or venal reasons.

The archdeacon (***erchdeken***) presided over the ecclesiastical court (***Court Cristien***) of first instance. Until the Council of Trent (1545-1563) remedied this dangerous situation, he had the power to impose excommunication for serious infringement of ecclesiastical laws or duties, for doctrinal deviation, and, with respect to the clergy, for any offense over which the ecclesiastical court had, or could seize, jurisdiction.

erchebisshop. A super-bishop, usually in the Middle Ages with authority over his own episcopal See (district) and supervisor over a province or collection of bishoprics. Although his powers were more or less limited beyond his own See, the office is of higher dignity and wider scope than bishop, though still, unless designated a cardinal archbishop, not an elector of the ***Pope***. Archbishops were appointed by the Pope, usually on the advice of the secular authority, though this was a recurring source of controversy.

Ester. 1. The Biblical Esther (Book of Esther). King Assuerus put aside his first wife and married the beautiful and powerless Esther, a Jewish exile under the care of her uncle Mordecai. At Mordecai's direction she gained favor with Assuerus by warning him of plots. She used her influence to prevent a massacre of the Jews. She is an intercessor on behalf of the chosen people and, therefore, a type of the Blessed Virgin Mary (***Marie, Seinte***). (See ***scripture***); 2. The feast of Easter, the celebration of the day Christ rose from the dead, the third day after His Crucifixion. The Resurrection is the confirmation of the truth and validity of Christ's revelation and is, as it was in the fourteenth century, considered the most important feast in the liturgical year. (See ***Crist.***)

Eva, Eve. The first woman, the wife of Adam, created either simultaneously with Adam (Gen. 1:26-27) or from Adam's rib (Gen. 2:21-23). The latter reading was favored in the Middle Ages, which saw Eve as secondary or subservient and most often, in writers in the anti-feminist tradition like St. Jerome, as a source of temptation and corruption. The anti-feminists blamed Eve for the Fall of Man from his state of original bliss in Paradise (Gen. 3:1-7). Women, seen as "daughters of Eve", were viewed as more corrupt and particularly more lascivious than men and thus a constant threat to male chastity and rectitude generally. The Blessed Virgin Mary (***Marie, Seinte***), the woman foretold who would crush the serpent, was the antidote or remedy to Eve.

evangile(s), evangelist, evaungelie, evaungelist. Strictly speaking the four evangelists, Matthew, Mark, Luke, and John, the writers of the four Gospels of the New Testament, but also the whole of the New Testament and, by extension, the preaching of the Gospel of the New Testament and the book itself. All variations imply divine authority and sacred reliability.

Ezechias, Ezechie. Hezekiah (2 Chron. 29-32) was credited with religious reforms including the purification of the temple and revival of the celebration of Passover. In the Book of Isaiah (38:10-20), he contracts a mortal illness, but is granted fifteen additional years of life. In his affliction he calls to God with some bitterness, but he is generally taken as an example of penitence rather than disaffection.

Ezechiel. The Biblical prophet, not to be confused with Hezekiah (***Ezechias***, ***Ezechie***). Ezekiel foretells divine punishment and retribution, but offers hope for a Messianic salvation after the predicted destruction. His emphasis is on heartfelt internal repentance for the evil ways of the Israelites. He is a model or type of penitence in that his prophetic message warns of sin's consequences and enjoins repentance as the only remedy. Even more than the other major prophets his emphasis is penitential.

faith, fayth, feith, feyth. Belief in God and trust in His Providence (***purveaunce***). Faith is one of the three theological virtues infused by God, though free will makes it possible for human beings to reject it or fall away from it. It is a gift of God, necessary for salvation, but requires an intellectual assent to a body of dogmatic beliefs. The resultant system is called "the faith", the body of knowledge that comes to be understood as orthodox religion itself. It is the sum of Scriptural revelation as understood in the light of Apostolic Tradition (teaching handed down from the original Apostles) and the "Magisterium" (the living teaching authority of the Church).

Two controversies surrounded faith in the Middle Ages. One concerned the question of knowledge: do human beings know by faith or reason or how much of our knowledge is attributable to either. Fideism, total reliance on faith, was seen not only as anti-intellectual but also a denigration of the rational capacity with which God had endowed human beings. Total reliance on reason, on the other hand, was seen as unwarrantable human pride and a rejection, at least implicit, of God's gift of faith. The poignant problem occurred when the conclusions of faith and reason seemed to be at odds with each other. Averroists, heretical disciples of the version of Aristotle taught by the Arab Averroes, argued that there were two truths and that they could exist simultaneously in contradiction. The great solution and synthesis for the Middle Ages was found in the theology of St. Thomas Aquinas, who acknowledged that not all things could be known by reason alone, that there were "mysteries", truths that were too deep to be discovered or fully fathomed by human reason, but whose acceptance was reasonable and amenable to rational explanation. For instance, God's existence could be known by the natural light of reason, but the Trinity could only be known by faith; that the world was created could be known by the natural light of reason, but that it would come to an end could only be known by faith; that the human soul was immortal could be known by the natural light of reason, but that it could enjoy the Beatific Vision (everlasting happiness, in heaven, contemplating God) could only be known by faith. Natural knowledge of God, the world, and the soul were "preambles" to faith, according to Aquinas, but the Trinity, the Second Coming of Christ, and the Beatific Vision were "articles" of faith proper. For those who grasped them, the preambles disposed people to faith and supported their faith, but for those who did not, faith in God, who can neither deceive nor be deceived, assured them of even the preambles. In fact, Aquinas indicates that the effects of ***sin*** (both original and actual) so muddle our minds, weaken our wills, and perturb our passions that only a few can reach what can be known naturally by reason, and then only after a long time, with "admixture of many errors" (ST I.1.1). In this sense, faith enables reason to exercise its fullest capacity. Thus faith and reason could be mutually supportive and not exist at odds with each other.

The second controversy was about whether salvation could be attained by faith alone or, as the heretical Pelagians argued, by good works. The controversy over faith and works had existed from the times of ***St. Paul*** and ***St. Augustine***. The Medieval synthesis, once again characteristically Thomistic, was that both were necessary, and that when St. Paul said that we are justified by "faith that lives in charity", he meant that faith was necessary for salvation, but that the gift of faith offered to man by God has to be accepted by man and made active in good deeds. Thus, the theological virtue was maintained and our responsibility for our actions was simultaneously affirmed.

fasting, fastyng(e). Abstaining from food or drink for designated periods of time or limiting the consumption of the amount of food and kind of drink. Fasting could be prescribed for a day, several days, or extended periods of time. Highly elaborate prescriptions for fasting existed throughout the Middle Ages, though an increased emphasis on fasting may have come as an influence from the Irish Church. It was always part of individual penitence—the so-called "mortification of the flesh"—and was incorporated into the rules of all monastic orders. Indeed, for ***monks*** fasting was a way of life, broken only on Sundays and feast days. In the early Church monks were permitted one meal on fast days, to be taken late in the day. By the fourteenth century, a noon meal was prescribed and a light evening meal was permitted. Meat was never to be taken except, at least according to the ***rule*** of St. Benedict (***Benedight***), when required for the health of an individual monk. However, fasting was also a regular discipline for the laity. In the early Church fasting was prescribed on the two days preceding Easter, and on Wednesdays and Fridays except during Eastertide.

Fasting was of three kinds in the fourteenth century. First, sacramental fasting was prescribed, for example, before reception of the Eucharist, and was often enjoined as a penitential obligation in the sacrament of Penance as satisfaction for sin. Second, seasonal fasting, limiting food intake to one main meal and a light meal to sustain strength, was prescribed during the penitential season of Lent and during Advent as preparation for the coming of the Redeemer at Christmas. Third, ascetic fasting was a monastic rule, a hermetic discipline, or any self-imposition for purposes of renunciation of the flesh. In all its forms, fasting was a familiar fact of life and a reminder of our obligation to subordinate and discipline all inclinations of the flesh.

fate. The inescapable predetermination of future events by a force or forces beyond our control. The belief that fate is absolute posed a problem for Christian thinkers, for if God is subject to fate, his power and freedom are limited in a way that seems incompatible with his divinity. If, on the other hand, God is the master of fate, he can foreknow our futures, but to the extent that this is true, there seems to be no room for us to choose freely and thus be praiseworthy or blameworthy. A limited fate, subject to God's control, however, is compatible with both God's divinity and human freedom. For instance, the sun may be fated to burn itself out and Jesus may be fated to return to earth at the end of time, but neither would, strictly speaking, be a limitation of human freedom of choice. (See ***fredom***, ***purveiaunce***.)

fe(e)nd. In the singular, Satan, the chief of the angels who rebelled against God and the tireless tempter of mankind away from God. In the plural, spirits from ***hell***, fallen angels, or any spiritual enemies. The sense of the reality of Satan and belief in infernal spirits was a clear and present part of the everyday life of the fourteenth century, so much so that the word was extended to apply to human beings who were ruthless and formidable enemies, who displayed the power and aspect of demons.

fermerer. The ***monk*** or friar (***frere***) in charge of the infirmary in a monastery or convent (***covent***) of male or female religious. His expertise did not necessarily even match the chancy medical skills of contemporary practicing doctors.

fe(e)ste. A large, celebratory consumption of food and drink, but in a religions sense the observance of special occasions: a holy day, a saint's day, or a day associated with a mystery or a major religious event. That feasting would be important is significant because laws of fasting were always suspended on feast days so they were an opportunity to eat and drink a lot. In a population that was largely poor, the celebratory and exceptional nature of feast days made them especially welcome. Also, in a world where paid vacations were unknown, it is small wonder that people rejoiced that there were over one hundred prescribed feast days over the course of a year.

fir of Seint Anthony. Erysipelas, gangrene, or any other virulent eruption of the skin. No particular connection with any St. Anthony is apparent.

fles(s)h. The flesh of man or beast, but, from the time of Christ and perhaps before, the aspect of man that has to do with the corporeal, therefore corruptible, as opposed to the spiritual and salvific. Christian tradition from ***St. Paul*** through ***Augustine*** and beyond opposed flesh to spirit as a way of life and as an attitude towards pleasure with a potential for corruption. Flesh represents the set of inclinations towards gratification of human desires, which must be subordinated to the will. The three great dangers to salvation were often cited in the Middle Ages as the World, the Flesh, and the Devil. Despite constant admonitions in sermons, people in the fourteenth century seem to have been rather more indulgent of sins of the flesh than one would expect in an age so permeated by religion.

for(e)knowynge. The knowledge that God has, if we are not to place limits on Him, of future events. Theologians attempted to reconcile this foreknowledge with free will, for if God knows what will happen, how can we be free to choose? Boethius (***Boece***) adverts to the problem, but the Medieval solution is in Aquinas and earlier scholastics, who argued that God does not force all human choices, but rather simply knows what they will be. Such theologians reasoned that mere (fore)knowledge on God's part is thus compatible with human freedom. Since God exists in eternity, *i.e.*, out of time, God's knowledge is not bound by time. All is present for Him at once; nothing is past or future. From a time-bound human perspective, however, God's eternal knowledge appears to be foreknowledge when it refers to what humans regard as the future. Necessarily, God timelessly knows what anyone will choose in time, but it is not the case that whatever is chosen, is chosen necessarily. That is, the necessity lies in the knowing, not in the choosing. A knotty problem remained, however, as to how Divine Providence (***purveaunce***) could operate in a world that included free will. (See ***fate***, ***fortune***.)

fornicacioun. Sexual transgressions including fornication proper (sexual intercourse between two unmarried people), adultery, concubinage, and any sexual activity by the clergy. The term was used in a broad sense to include any sexual intercourse outside of marriage and, according to some commentators, could include sex within marriage when there was not the proper intention of the procreation of children. The rules were complex, but behavior was usually treated with understanding except for clergy, who were frequently satirized in this regard.

fortitudo. Although this is a Latin word used only by the Parson and immediately defined by him as a remedy against the deadly sin of sloth (***slouthe***), it requires special note because fortitude is one of the four cardinal moral virtues. It is a kind of strength or determination or endurance in the avoidance of sin and the living of the Christian life. (See ***vertu***.)

fortune. Chance or accident rather than fate or design or the operation of free will (***fredom***). The pagan goddess Fortuna was commonly invoked as an allegorical figure for this force for unpredictability. The idea of fortune became involved in the controversies about fate, free will, and God's foreknowledge. The fickleness of fortune was invoked as a reason for *contemptus mundi*, a distrust of the things of this world most notably demonstrated in the monastic life. The "wheel of fortune", on which human beings are sometimes up and sometimes down, was often cited as a reason to distrust wealth and happiness as transient. A more orthodox explanation of this ephemerality argued that what seems from a human point of view to be fortune is simply, *sub specie aeternitatis*, the inevitable working out of God's providential plan. (See ***aventure***, ***fate, purveaunce***.)

foryevenesse, foryifnesse. The forgiving of sin, accomplished through contrition, confession, and acts of satisfaction for sin, and effected by priestly ***absolution*** in the ***sacrament*** of ***Penance***. Sin was taken seriously, but so was the opportunity for recovery from sin as a prime doctrine of the Christian doctrine of Redemption. The "Parson's Tale" is a long and noteworthy exposition on the subject. Original sin disposed man to sin, but the sacrifice of Christ made possible, granted the prosper disposition, forgiveness and moral regeneration.

fredom, fredam. The human faculty of choice. Free will is necessary if human beings are to be responsible for their own sins. Free will can be diminished according to Aquinas, by a pattern of choices of lesser goods, but it can never entirely be removed. That is, repeated choices can become so habitual that one's future freedom to choose otherwise is impaired. In any case, the human will is not entirely free, although by definition it is always voluntary: Aquinas holds that we necessarily (and yet voluntarily) will our own happiness as our ultimate end, but we are free to choose rightly or wrongly among various means to that happiness. (See ***fate***, ***purveaunce***.)

FRER(E). A friar (from the French, ultimately Latin, for "brother") is a member of one of the mendicant orders. Mendicants are religious who characteristically live outside the confines of a monastery or nunnery, who support themselves by begging (*mendicans* is Latin for "beggar", ***begger***), that is, by preaching the Gospel and living off the alms of the faithful. Mendicant friars take vows of poverty, chastity, and obedience (to Church authority generally and to their prior in particular), with a strong emphasis on poverty. In Chaucer's time, they could not even hold property in common as the monastic orders could. Although they did congregate at communal houses, usually called convents (**covent**), they did not withdraw from the world but moved about more freely than monks and nuns, fulfilling their mission by preaching the Gospel and surviving by charity. Because they were not under the permanent authority of a local bishop, they often provoked hostility among secular clergy, especially when their more radical poverty occasioned invidious comparisons with the relative affluence of other ecclesiastics. Friars, by eschewing status in their communal life of poverty, chastity, and obedience, are to exemplify the equality of all men as brothers. Thus a friar who publicly sins by pride or vanity is particularly scandalous.

There were four mendicant orders during Chaucer's time. Perhaps the best known because of their high intellectual tradition, the Dominicans, called Blackfriars because of the black mantle they wore over their white habit, were founded by St. Dominic in 1215. They were generally esteemed, and maybe feared, as the most learned order, producing some of the major scholars of the Middle Ages. Properly known as the Order of Preachers (O.P.), the Dominicans are the order of Thomas Aquinas and Albertus Magnus. The Franciscans, called Grayfriars because of their habit, were founded by St. Francis of Assisi in 1209 and confirmed by the Pope in 1223. They were renowned for their self-denial and generosity, and were probably the most austere in their commitment to poverty. The Carmelites, or White Friars, were founded as a primarily contemplative order but became mendicants in 1245. The Augustinians (***Augustyns***), Austin Friars, traced their origins to ***St. Augustine*** of Hippo but were confirmed as an establishment by the amalgamation of various bodies of hermits by Pope Honorius III in 1226.

Mendicant orders flourished in the thirteenth century, but by the fourteenth century enough abuses had crept into the ideal so that the fat friar, corrupt and lascivious and greedy, became a familiar object of satire. Unsavory friars, willing to enrich themselves and deceive the faithful as in Chaucer's "General Prologue" and "Friar's Tale" and in Langland's *Piers Plowman*, had become regrettably common figures, despite recurrent papal admonitions to them to reform.

FURTHER READING: Rosalind Brooke, *The Coming of the Friars* (London: G. Allen and Unwin, 1975); C. H. Lawrence, *The Friars: The Impact of the Early Mendicant Movement on Western Society* (London: Longman, 1994).

Frere Menour. A Franciscan friar, *i.e.* a member of the Order of Friars Minor, founded by St. Francis in 1209 with a radical commitment to poverty and preaching the Gospel. (See ***frere***.)

Freres Prechours. Dominican friars. Members of the Order of Preachers founded by St. Dominic in 1215. Called Blackfriars because of their black mantle over a white habit, the Dominicans developed a dominant reputation for preaching, teaching, and learning and counted many of the major scholars of the Middle Ages among their number. (See ***frere***.)

Frydeswyde, Seint. St. Frideswide (cr. 650-735) was a virgin and the patron of Oxford. Frideswide fled from marriage with King Algar of Mercia and founded a monastery. Her fame grew with the increasing prominence of Oxford, and students processed to her shrine twice a year.

The history of her bodily remains, subsequent to our period, is more interesting than the few facts we have about her life. A victim of Reformation body-moving, her remains were ultimately mixed with those of a certain Catherine Cathie, an ex-nun who ran off with an ex-friar, during the reign of Elizabeth I.

Gabrielles. The genitive of the name of the ***archangel*** Gabriel, the archangel who announced to Mary that she would be the mother of Christ (Luke 1:26-38). Gabriel was, consequently, associated with the Incarnation of ***Christ*** and His sacrificial ***Redemption*** of man from Adam's original sin. An archangel was not the highest among the nine choirs of ***angels***, but was the most notable of Biblical messengers usually assuming human form in order to communicate. In the Hebrew Scriptures Gabriel was associated with the power of God and it is he who is expected to blow the final trumpet signaling the end of the world. In the Christian Scriptures, Gabriel is more associated with consolation and mercy and his final trumpet, though fearful, heralds the Second Coming of Christ.

Galilee. A mountainous but productive region of Palestine. It is Jesus' native land as His birthplace, Nazareth, was the major city in the southern part of the province. In Galilee Jesus began his public ministry and it is the locale in which most of Jesus' activities are reported by the synoptic gospels of Matthew, Mark and Luke.

Gazan. The Biblical city of Gaza was one of the oldest cities in the world. Conquered and ruled by the Philistines, the perennial Gentile antagonists of the Jews, it was assigned to the tribe of Judah, by Mosaic decree if not in fact, when Moses and the Hebrews arrived. Gaza is the city to which the blinded Samson (***Sampson***) was taken after his entrapment by Delilah (***Dalida***) and where he destroyed the temple in an astonishing demonstration of his returned strength (Judges 16).

Gile, Seint. St. Giles or Aegidius was born of a rich and noble Athenian family in the middle of the seventh century. Thus he is another of the saints from the hazy past who are accorded aristocratic forbears, perhaps to make their commitment to Christianity all the more impressive. He withdrew to Gaul and founded a monastery following the ***rule*** of St. Benedict (***Benedight***). He was known for holiness and simplicity of life, despite offers of wealth and honor. His cult spread rapidly after his death and quite soon many churches were named for him. (See ***seint***.)

glose. To interpret or explain, especially a sacred text. By extension it was applied to commentary, originally marginal, on any text, and even developed the pejorative implication of "to gloss over".

Glossing texts has a long history. Greek grammarians defined words that needed clarification and later glossing tended to explain the explanations. In Christian use it was most frequently applied to exegesis of Scripture whether marginal or interlinear and was often a vehicle for fourfold allegorical interpretation. The most famous gloss of the Middle Ages was the *Glossa Ordinaria* of Strabo (d. 849), which illustrated various senses, especially the literal, of the Bible. Strabo was a revered source for Aquinas. Of almost equal renown was Anselm of Laon's (d. 1117) *Glossa Interlinearis*. Copies of the Vulgate Bible usually had both marginal and interlinear glosses.

glotenye, glotonye. One of the seven deadly sins (***deedly synnes***). Gluttony was overindulgence in food or drink. Although usually not considered very serious, it was one of the so-called "tavern sins" with which itinerant preachers found it useful to belabor the simple folk. The illustrations could be entertaining and the moral lesson personally poignant since it was likely one of the more common human failings.

Goddes bones. A mild oath invoking the bones of Christ. If it was a blasphemy (***blasphemynge***), it was a mild or thoughtless one frequently used in popular parlance.

Goddes privite, pryvete(e), pryvyte, Privitee was any kind of secrecy or privacy, but God's privacy signified the knowledge that is appropriate only to God. For human beings to inquire into it was to exceed the proper bounds of human limitation. Alchemists, magicians, and just plain charlatans of all sorts aspired to this kind of knowledge and therefore intruded, inappropriately and sinfully, on what should remain the province of the divine. Some matters are beyond proper human understanding and to inquire into them or pretend a knowledge of them is sinful and dangerous. Hence, the clerks in the "Miller's Tale" and the "Franklin's Tale" and the canon in the "Canon's Yeoman's Tale" are on very shaky ground.

Golias. Goliath of Geth (1 Sam. 17) was a giant Philistine warrior. While David was with Saul fighting the Philistines, Goliath challenged the Israelites to single combat and was defeated by David, the young harper and later king, with his famous slingshot. David thus became a type of the religious person, later the Christian, confronting the formidable power of Satan or sin. (See ***scripture***.)

gospel. From the Old English god-spell, good news, gospel refers to the books of the four evangelists—Matthew, Mark, Luke, and John—or to the New Testament in its entirety as the reporting of the life and teachings of ***Christ***.

grace, gras. Grace is a complex spiritual version of the more secular imposition of the word that has to do with favor or benefit. It is a supernatural gift or favor, unmerited, communicated by the Holy Ghost manifesting his aspect as Divine Love.

There are two kinds of grace. Sanctifying or habitual grace is a raising of our nature, a kind of supernatural adoption which gives new birth and life to the soul and makes ***salvation*** possible. Actual grace is a transient gift that enlightens the mind and moves the will to empower Christians to avoid sin and do the good. Most clearly expounded by Aquinas, grace is an indwelling of the Holy Ghost, an inhering quality, that makes virtuous action and salvation accessible to human beings. Aquinas explains that grace is itself efficacious, but free will consents because grace effectively premoves it to the performance of the good.

Gregorie, Seint. St. Gregory the Great (c. 540-604) was Pope from 590 to 604. A revered reformer and teacher, he is a Doctor of the Church and influenced the doctrine, organization, and discipline of the Church. Most significant principles of Medieval Christianty are, at least basically, discussed in Gregory. From liturgy, to Church relations, to the prerogatives of the Papacy, to Church governance and relations with secular political entities, Gregory was a powerful force. The single most important figure in the formation of the Medieval Church, he was not a philosopher or theologian so much as a lawyer, administrator, preacher, and leader. Even after election to the Papacy, which he clearly established as the decisive authority in the Church, Gregory lived as a ***monk*** according to the ***rule*** of St. Benedict (***Benedight***). He was canonized by acclamation almost immediately after his death, formal procedures for canonization having not yet been established.

halwes. As a verb to "halwen" the word means to make holy. Thus "halwes" are saints, those who have achieved ***salvation*** and therefore are capable of acting as intercessors with God in response to the prayers of the faithful. They cannot grant spiritual favors in their own right, though miracles are and must be attributed to them for formal canonization. They are in a privileged position to petition God. All of the saved are saints, but official recognition by the Church through the process of canonization provides the authority for invoking them. The number of saints mentioned by Chaucer suggests the importance of their role in Medieval Christianity even when their names are present simply as mild oaths. (See ***seint***.)

harwed. Harrowed refers to the story of the "harrowing of hell", popular in the Middle Ages, according to which Christ visited hell between His Crucifixion and His Resurrection. At this time He freed the souls of the Old Testament patriarchs and, according to some versions, notable people who had lived good lives, and according to an even more benign version freed all those who had died before the Incarnation. The doctrine is loosely based on the New Testament and the teachings of the Fathers of the Church with some details from the apocryphal Gospel of Nicodemus.

Helie. Eli (esp. 1 Samuel 1-4) was a Biblical judge and high priest. In his old age he was weak and indulgent to his sons whose crimes brought ruin on them. He died at 98 when he heard that his two sons had been killed and the Ark of the Covenant had been seized by the Philistines. Eli appears as kind and wise, but made foolish by his soft behavior towards his sons. (See ***scripture***.)

helle. The place, and indeed a specific location was meant, of eternal punishment from which there is no escape or release for eternity. From Old English "helan", a dark or hidden place, a hole or cavern, hell was often conceived of as beneath the earth, but this was probably metaphorical even by the time of Dante. Dante places over the gateway to hell the inscription "Abandon all hope, you who enter here", and explains that hell was created as a manifestation of God's wisdom and justice. Divine justice requires eternal punishment for serious sin because it is an offense against the infinite love and authority of God. The souls in hell suffer dual punishment: the pain of fire or physical torment, and the greater pain of loss, which comes from the recognition that they are forever separated from God, the goal of their existence. Thus, human life becomes a period of moral probation after which an inexorable judgment is made. The idea of hell was a frequent motif of Medieval preachers both hortatory and extortionate.

heremyte, hermyte. A recluse who has withdrawn into solitude to live the perfection of the Christian life, sometimes called an anchorite or eremite. Eremitism was an early form of non-communal monastic seclusion. ***St. Anthony*** of Egypt brought on the vogue in the fourth century, though such behavior has antecedents in the Hebrew Scriptures and John the Baptist is said to have lived like a hermit. Hermits were mostly an Eastern phenomenon in the deserts of Egypt, Syria, and the Sinai. There was a running debate over eremitic (solitary) versus cenobitic (communal) monasticism, and, although the Church approved of all renunciation of this world, it generally preferred the alternative of monastic communities. (See ***monk***.)

HERESYE. A deviation from the dogmatic teaching of the Church. A heresy could be "material", a mere error in the interpretation of doctrine or, more culpably, "formal", persistence in error despite correction by a legitimate teaching authority. Although heresy is different from blasphemy (***blasphemynge***), a challenge to or rebellion against God, blasphemy is often included as a variety of heresy because it is behavior antithetical to the foundation of Christian belief. Aquinas (*Summa Theologica* II-II.11.1) describes heresy as "a species of unbelief, belonging to those who profess the Christian faith, but corrupt its dogmas". Heresy involves rejection of part of the totality of Church teaching as opposed to apostasy, which is an entire abandonment of and disregard for the faith, or schism, which is a denial of the authority of the ***Pope***. Heretics are also different from infidels or heathens, who have never accepted the faith and been baptized. In the Middle Ages heresy could, however, be generalized to be flagrant moral corruption or disregard for moral law.

From the earliest days of Christianity, challenges arose to such fundamental doctrines as the Trinity, the divinity of Christ, original sin, and the necessity of grace. In opposition to a plethora of deviations, apologists for orthodox beliefs, from Origen and Tertullian (who themselves eventually fell victim to heresies) through Ambrose and Augustine to Aquinas and the Scholastics, helped to develop the body of sanctioned Christian belief. Indeed, in one sense, the history of heresy is intimately bound up with the formulation and articulation of the body of orthodox Christian doctrine. This process continued beyond the Middle Ages, notably in the Roman Catholic Church's response to the Reformation at the Council of Trent (1545-1563).

Although the variety of heresy was manifold, several exemplary early heresies seem worthy of mention because of their persistence in various forms. The first major heresy, Arianism, arose in the second century and denied the divinity of Christ, thereby impugning both the Trinity and the idea of Redemption, which depends upon the suffering and death of a Christ who is both human and divine. In the third century, Manichaeism, a descendant of ancient Zoroastrian cults, argued that there was a continual conflict between a principle of good (God, light) and a principle of evil (the Devil, darkness), and that man and the universe were the creation of the evil principle. Most effectively combated by St. Augustine, himself long a Manichaean catechumen, this heresy survived in many versions of a good-evil dichotomy through the Cathars, who professed a radical puritanism by withdrawing from what they saw to be an intrinsically evil world created by the evil force, even up to the Albigensians, who professed a similar belief with great success in twelfth and thirteenth century France. In the fifth century, Pelagians, by denying original sin, argued that good works were possible without grace. Once again, St. Augustine came to the rescue, but variations on the controversy over salvation by faith or works have persisted throughout much of Church history.

Fourteenth-century England was relatively free of significant heresy (though the danger was continually cited by popular preachers) until the emergence of the Lollards (***Lollere***), disciples of John Wyclif, towards the end of the century. Lollards challenged the instrumentality of the clergy, and thereby the efficacy of sacraments, and also asserted the primacy of

Scripture over Church tradition. Wyclif was convicted of heresy by the London Synod of 1382.

The religious term was appropriated in a curious and amusing way by the courtly love tradition, which applied it to those who did not subscribe or submit to the power of the god of love.

FURTHER READING: Gordon Leff, *Heresy in the Later Middle Ages* (Manchester: Manchester University Press, 1967); Malcolm D. Lambert, *Medieval Heresy*, 2nd edn. (Cambridge, MA: B. Blackwell, 1992).

Herodes. In Matthew 2, astrologers from the East tell Herod the Great that they have come because of the prophecy of the birth of a greater king. Of a brutal and wholly secular turn of mind, Herod ordered the murder of every male under the age of two in Bethlehem, the so-called slaughter of the innocents. Joseph, on the advice of an angel, had prudently taken Mary and Jesus to the safety of Egypt, but not before the astrologers worshipped Jesus and prudently returned home by a different route.

Herod Antipas (Mark 6:14-29) imprisoned John the Baptist but was afraid to kill him. Living incestuously with Herodias, his brother's wife, the profligate Herod was pleased by the dancing of Herodias' daughter, Salome, and offered her a gift. At the instigation of her mother she asked for and received the head of John the Baptist.

hethen(e), hethenesse. A pagan, indeed a thorough-going pagan since heathen could refer to all who were neither Christians nor Jews. Heathens, because of their total ignorance of or resistance to Christianity or even the Old Law of the Hebrews, were considered particularly brutal with a barbaric hostility towards Christians. "Hethenesse", thus, would be lands of godlessness and idolatry with neither justice nor mercy, as opposed to Christendom, the world under Christ's revelation. This attitude did not dissuade Christians from imposing forced conversions on conquered heathens from the beginning of the Crusades, apparently out of a conviction that the souls of the pagans could be saved by brute force.

heven(e). The place, and like hell it was indeed considered a place, of ***salvation***. Although spoken of as above the earth, the specific location was not dogmatically identified. More important was that it was the place of beatitude, of reward for those who had lived in grace and been faithful to God's revelation. Representations of heaven are generally rather airy, nebulous places, though they are sometimes represented in poetry as a glorious city, recognizably Medieval. Conceptually, however, the essential reward of heaven was the beatific vision, an immediate perception of God, the end and greatest good of our existence, which transcends the natural power of the human intellect. After the Second Coming of Christ, the souls of the saved were to be reunited with their bodies now in a new and improved form.

Holi, Ho(o)ly Go(o)st. The third person of the Blessed Trinity. The Holy Ghost, or Holy Spirit, is coeval and consubstantial with the Father and the Son in the triadic "three person-one God" theology of the Trinity (***trinitee***). The Holy Ghost was said to "proceed" from the everlasting love of the Father and Son. Objections to and misunderstandings of the Trinity arose early in the Church and heretics, most notably the Arians, denied that the Holy Ghost was a separate person, distinct from the Father and the Son. Nevertheless, the Trinity has consistently been an article of faith, a necessary dogma, and has been analyzed from St. Augustine's *De Trinitate*, through Aquinas and the Scholastics, to William of Ockham who in the early fourteenth century argued that the Trinity could only be known by faith not by reason, and beyond in continuing controversies.

The Holy Ghost, because of the manner of "procession", from the love between the Father and the Son, is most often associated with Divine Love. Even though all three persons share all divine attributes, the Father is most often associated with power, the Son with wisdom, and the Holy Spirit with the divine love manifested in the operations of grace and the sanctification of souls. The seven gifts of the Holy Ghost, as the Spirit works on our souls through grace, are wisdom, understanding, counsel, fortitude, knowledge, piety, and fear of the Lord.

hope. Hope, with faith and charity, is a theological virtue (***vertu***) and therefore a divine infusion rather than a merited consolation of existence. It is the desire for ***salvation*** and the reasonable expectation of achieving it involving a recognition of our responsibility to behave properly and believe in the reality of God's mercy. Its opposite, ***despair***, is the anguished and erroneous belief that our sins are too great or, as the heretical Albegensians believed, that God does not grant forgiveness for sin.

Hospitaliers, Hospitelers. Most notably the Hospitallers of St. John of Jerusalem, perhaps the most important of all the military monastic orders. The Hospitallers emerged before the Crusades to serve pilgrims to the Holy

Land and to minister to the sick, though they were officially established by a bull of Pope Paschal II in 1113 to their founder, Gerald or Gerard. His successor, Robert of Provence (1120-1160), erected buildings near the Church of the Holy Sepulchre in Jerusalem. This hospice became a community composed of "military brothers" and "infirmarians", those primarily devoted to the care of the sick. Essentially the Hospitallers became "warrior monks" who retained their tradition of hospitality and care for the sick. Like the ***Templars***, the Hospitallers lived by a version of the ***rule*** of St. Benedict (***Benedight***). Though not such a furious military entity as the Templars were reputed to be, they were of the same ecclesiastical rank and grew increasingly warlike, even to the point of causing some concern in Rome. From 1309 they became known as the Knights of Malta although their old name survived in common usage. When the Templars were disbanded, those warrior monks were given the option of joining the Hospitallers, which many of them did.

Houly Writ. The Bible; the Hebrew and Christian ***Scriptures*** probably including for the Middle Ages the books that have come to be called apocryphal as well as those that have remained canonical.

Hugh of Lincoln. Hugh of Lincoln was considered a martyr in the fourteenth century. Although there is no documentary evidence, Child Ballad 155, "Sir Hugh and the Jew's Daughter", preserves the legend of his martyrdom by Jews in 1255. He was listed as a saint until recently and a plaque to him in Lincoln Cathedral was only removed in 1959. Whether he existed or not, Hugh was an object of sentimental devotion in the fourteenth century.

It is hard not to think of the authentic St. Hugh of Lincoln (1135-1200), a Carthusian, who had the courage even after the unfortunate experience of ***St. Thomas*** a Becket to reprove Henry II. St. Hugh established the first Carthusian house in England (1180), became Bishop of Lincoln (1181), and rebuilt the cathedral (1185). He was canonized in 1220.

indulgence. Although there is a strictly religious definition of this word, famous in the history of Christianity, Chaucer only uses it as permission or understanding or forgiveness. For the more technical sense, remission of all or part of the temporal (***purgatorial***) punishment due to sin, Chaucer uses the word ***pardoun***.

Innocent. Innocent III (c. 1160-1216) was Pope from 1198-1216. A learned theologian and supporter of the Crusades, he forcefully asserted Papal prerogatives especially power over the election of the Holy Roman Emperor. Indeed, he argued Papal rights and authority over all of Europe. He was a vigorous opponent of the Albigensians, a neo-Manichaean heretical group that arose from the Catharists and flourished in Southern France in the twelfth and thirteenth centuries. Albigensians believed in a radical duality between good and evil; the corruption of the body was so great (it was the creature of the evil force) that they countenanced suicide and sodomy in preference to procreation. (See ***heresye***.)

In Principio. The first words, in Latin, of Genesis and of St. John's Gospel. It was a popular Medieval religious phrase, probably because of the symmetry it implied between the first book of the Hebrew ***Scriptures*** and the last of the four evangelists of the Christian Scriptures.

invidie. The deadly sin of envy (***envie***). Invidie is simply a transliteration of the Latin "invidia". (See ***deedly synnes***.)

ire. The deadly sin of ***anger*** or wrath, ire is a violent and irrational loss of control. Although anger can be justified or mitigated and righteous anger can even be laudable, ire, a transliteration of the Latin "ira", is both the act and the underlying disposition that produces excess in what might otherwise be permissible or proper. (See ***deedly synnes***.)

Israel. Both the land of Israel and the people of Israel, the descendants of the Biblical patriarch ***Jacob***. Through strife and dispossession, it is the kingdom of God's chosen people, the Jews. (See ***scripture***.)

Jacob. The third in the line of the great Biblical patriarchs after ***Abraham*** and ***Isaac*** (Gen. 24:28-34, 25, 27). Jacob was the immediate ancestor of the twelve tribes of Israel. Having secured the blessing of Isaac with the assistance of his mother, Rebecca (***Rebekka***) at the expense of his elder twin Esau, he became the direct forbear of the people of Israel. With Jacob, God renewed the covenant that he had made with Abraham and Isaac. (See ***scripture***.)

Jacobyn. A Dominican friar. The name was originally only applied to French Dominicans. It derived from the Church of St. Jacques, which was donated to the Dominicans and where they built their first convent (their name for their communal dwelling).

Founded in 1208 by St. Dominic, the Dominicans were at their height in the thirteenth century. The order that produced such distinguished scholars as Aquinas and Albertus Magnus, the Dominicans took learning and preaching as their main roles. Although strictly speaking mendicants, the order allowed great leeway in the vow of poverty to allow for the effective pursuit of scholarship and teaching. They allowed no convent to exist without a Doctor as well as an administrative authority. Their conventual schools, which taught Scripture and theology and, later, philosophy, spread across Europe. From the beginning they were constituted as an order of clerics so that they could both supplement the slender number of secular clergy and train new clerics in orthodox doctrine.

Jame, Seint. 1. The Apostle St. James the Greater, son of Zebedee and brother of ***John***, "the apostle whom Jesus loved". Some commentators think James and John were cousins of Jesus; they were called the "sons of thunder" (Luke 3:17). James and John were, along with Peter, privileged among the apostles; for example, they were present at the Transfiguration of Christ (Matt. 17:1-17). St. James is thought to have preached in Spain and to have been martyred in 44 by Herod Agrippa; 2. The Shrine of St. James (Santiago) Compostela in Spain whither the body of St. James the Apostle was believed to have been translated. It was, with Canterbury, one of the major European destinations for ***pilgrimages***; 3. St. James, the author of the Epistle, probably bishop of Jerusalem (Acts 15). The authenticity of his epistle was accepted by St. Jerome **(Jeremie)** and, although considered deuterocanonical, it gained acceptance by the fourteenth century

Jepte. Jephthah was a warrior and the son of a harlot. He vowed to sacrifice (*i.e.*, kill) whoever was first to come out of his house (Judges 11:1-12:7). Unfortunately, it turned out to be his daughter, who requested a reprieve of two months to lament her wasted virginity. His story is an instructive lesson concerning rash vows with terrible consequences and uncomfortably suggests the practice of human sacrifice among the Jews. However, Jephthah was not truly a Jew, but an outlaw recruited to fight against the Ammonites. (See ***scripture***.)

Jeremeye. The Biblical prophet Jeremiah, one of the four "major" prophets. A contemporary of Solon and Draco, he lived during a period of political and military confusion in Western Asia. He is particularly the prophet of mourning and suffering on a mission from God to proclaim that Jerusalem and the Temple would be overthrown, the so-called "catastrophe of Zion". Jeremiah appeared in public in chains to dramatize his prophecies of impending captivity. His view is black indeed in that he sees catastrophe as a moral necessity and a visitation on the people for their failure to observe the Mosaic Law. Almost needless to say, his prophecies, delivered in a simple, vigorous, and agonized style, antagonized his own people, who rejected him and even threatened physical violence. His is the tortured voice of a man suffering the inevitability of destruction and the futility of his prophecy. Also, he apparently did not feel very well.

Jeremie, Jeremye, Seint. St. Jerome (c. 340-420) was the translator of the Bible into Latin known as the Vulgate, the form in which the Bible was available for most of the Middle Ages. He wrote voluminously: exegeses of the Bible, theological controversy, history, letters, and other translations. His scriptural commentary is often allegorical and was a prime model for those who advocated fourfold interpretation during the Middle Ages.

His treatise *Adversus Jovinianum* was an attack, as his theological writings tended to be, on Jovinianus, a Pelagian (an exponent of the heretical belief that man is saved entirely by works), who denied that virginity was a higher state than marriage and defended marital sex and a generally more relaxed view of how to live the Christian life. In his response, St. Jerome defends asceticism and incorporates savage attacks on marriage and women. Thereby he became one of the favorite "authorities" of the anti-feminists who saw all women as tempting and lascivious "daughters of Eve". *Adversus Jovinianum* does contain the only extant version of an anti-feminist tract by Theophrastus, "The Golden Book of Marriage". After all, St. Jerome, irascible, sarcastic, and contentions, was a better translator and controversialist than theologian.

Jerusalem. Jerusalem was the principal city of the Jews; it was both a political capital and a religious locus of prime importance throughout the history of the Israelites. Its history has been turbulent. As ancient "Salem" it was the kingdom of the priest Melchisedech, but was conquered by the Chaldeans. After the time of Abraham it passed into the possession of Egypt. When the Jews reached the promised land, Jerusalem was assigned to the tribe of Benjamin. About 1058 B.C.E., it was conquered by David and he restored the Ark of the Covenant to the city which thereafter became known as "the city of David". It was captured and the Temple destroyed by the Romans in 71 C.E.

Jerusalem became a sacred place for Christians. It was the Holy Land, the place where ***Christ*** was crucified and rose again for the ***Redemption*** of mankind. As early as 420, St. Jerome reports that it was a destination for religious pilgrims from all over the known world. By the eighth century conquest by the Arabs continued its troubled history, and its recovery became the reason for the Crusades, for Christians viewed it as peculiarly the "city of God". So important was the city that "the new Jerusalem" became a name and allegorical type for the heavenly kingdom.

Jewerye, Juerie. The Jewish nation, the Jewish people, or a Jewish ghetto. Anti-Semitism was rife in the Middle Ages. Jews had been expelled from England in the late thirteenth century, but Anti-Semitism persisted. The popular conception of Jews as "Christ killers" overwhelmed traditional Christian perceptions of Judaism as the forerunner of Christianity.

Jhesu(s); Jesu(s) (Christ), Crist, Xristus. The second person of the Blessed Trinity Incarnate. Jesus is a Latin form derived via Greek from the Hebrew Joshua. Christ or Chistos is the equivalent of the Hebrew "Messiah", "the anointed one". Jesus' Incarnation required that He be one person (and that person a member of the Blessed Trinity) and possess two natures—one divine and one human. As early as the fourth century Arians denied the divinity of Christ, but His membership in the Trinity and His assumption of a human as well as a divine nature in the Incarnation were both unchallengeable articles of orthodox Christianity in the fourteenth century. In the Christian scheme Christ's primary role was the ***Redemption*** of man by His suffering and crucifixion and His confirmation of His message by means of His Resurrection.

The centrality of Christ as Redeemer to the Christian revelation virtually assured that His name would be used in blasphemies, mild oaths, and pious ejaculations. (See ***Crist***.)

Jhesu Nazarenus Rex Judeorum. Jesus of Nazareth, King of the Jews. Pontius Pilate had a sign inscribed in Latin (as here), Greek, and Hebrew and affixed to the Cross (John 19:19-22) despite the objections of the chief priests of the Jews. Abbreviated as INRI it became a symbol of Jesus' misunderstood claims to kingship.

Jhesu (filius) Syrak. Jesus, son of Sirach, was the author of Ecclesiasticus, a book of the Old Testament not canonical to the Hebrew Scriptures. Sometimes called the Book of Sirach, it is a complilation of wise sayings and advice. By the fourteenth century Christians who accepted its canonicity tended to call it Ecclesiasticus.

Joab. A general in David's army who sounds his trumpet to direct his army (2 Samuel) especially in the battle against the Benjaminites (2 Samuel 2:28, 18:16, and 20:22). He was a formidable defender of David during David's bad times.

Job. The central figure of the Biblical Book of Job. He lived far to the East and was not one of the chosen people, though this is usually ignored in commentary on the significance of the story. A successful and upright man, he is assaulted by Satan with six great trials. He suffers loss of property, the death of kin, and physical debilities while three "comforters" alternate between self-righteous commentary blaming Job and misguided advice to Job to rebel against God, Who is allowing Satan (***Sathan***) to execute these trials. Although Job is tempted to complain to God about His treatment of him, he ultimately resists, seems to accept some responsibility, and assigns the rest to our inability to comprehend God. A bystander, Eliu, resolves the issues with prophetic analysis; suffering, deserved or undeserved, promotes virtue and the behavior of the Divinity is inscrutable.

By the Middle Ages Job had become the proverbial model for patience in adversity.

Joce. St. Judicius (d. 699) was a Breton saint about whom little is known. He has a tenuous link with the *Canterbury Tales* by virtue of the fact that he is pictured with a pilgrim's staff and his relics were preserved at Hyde Abbey, whose abbot owned the Tabard and had lodgings nearby.

John (Johan), Seint. 1. The Evangelist or "the Divine", author of the fourth Gospel of the New Testament. There has been some controversy over who he was and was not. He was the son of Zebedee and Salome, and the brother of the Apostle James the Greater. A disciple initially of John the Baptist, he became one of the privileged apostles allowed, with ***Peter*** and ***James***, to view the Transfiguration of ***Christ*** (a visual manifestation of His divinity) and His agony in the garden of Gethsemane. His Gospel, of interest more for what Jesus says than does, concentrates on the person of the Redeemer rather than His miraculous ministry. The Middle Ages also believed that he was the author of three Epistles and the Book of Revelation, that highly symbolic vision of the end times; modern scholars disagree. John was believed to have taught in Asia after the dispersal of the Apostles by the persecutions of ***Herod Agrippa***. According to some authorities he was a cousin of Jesus and is identified in ***Scripture*** as the "disciple whom Jesus loved"; 2. John the Baptist, the son of Mary's cousin Elizabeth, who conceived late in her life. Luke's Gospel gives the most complete account of the Baptist's ministry. Six months older than Jesus, he was seen as the precursor or forerunner of Christ, living a wild semi-eremitic existence, baptizing with water, and preaching in preparation for the public ministry of Jesus and proclaiming that Jesus is the long-awaited Messiah. Jesus confirmed John as the greatest of the prophets, and an early and widespread devotion to him emerged. He was imprisoned and beheaded by ***Herod Antipas***.

John Crisostom, Seint. St. John Chrysostom (c. 347-407) was the most prominent Father and Doctor of the Greek Church. After two years as an anchorite, he returned to Antioch and, preaching in a time of various and confusing heresies, argued effectively against various Gnostics and Manichaeans. He became Bishop of Constantinople in 398 and instituted wide-ranging ecclesiastical and liturgical reforms. Though deposed through a hostile intrigue and never restored to his episcopacy, he was a prolific writer of homilies, anti-heretical apologetics, and scriptural commentary, though his traditional reputation has been as a gifted orator, Chrysostom meaning "Golden Mouth".

Jonas. The fifth of the minor prophets, in the Book of Jonah he is commanded to go to Nineveh, but tries to avoid his mission by going to Tarsus. On the way his ship is wrecked and he is swallowed by a large fish and disgorged unharmed on dry land three days later. Following a second command, he acts out a more traditional prophetic role predicting the destruction of the city, whereupon the leaders dictate repentance. Jonah is in fact disappointed and says that this was why he tried to avoid preaching in Nineveh; it did not deserve to be saved.

In the Hebrew Scriptures he is both a successful prophet and an example of how it is impossible to circumvent God's will. For Christians his three days' sojourn in the fish was a prefigurement of Christ's three days of burial. The similitude is made clear by ***Christ*** Himself (Matt. 12:40-41 and

16:4; Luke 11:29-32) when He says that the only sign the people will get will be the sign of Jonah and thus it will be with the Son of Man, Christ. That is, Christ's three days in the grave and His Resurrection will be the only confirmation of His message.

Joseph. In the Hebrew Scriptures (Gen. 30, 37, 39) Joseph was the eleventh son of ***Jacob*** and the first-born of ***Rachel***. Favored by his father, he was hated by his brothers. Jacob gave him a "coat of many colors", which intensified the envy of his brothers. They dipped the coat in sheep's blood, pretended that he had been killed, and sold him into slavery in Egypt. His natural gifts impressed Potiphar and Joseph was made supervisor and advisor. However, the thwarted wife of Potiphar accused Joseph of adultery with her and he was imprisoned.

He gained his release by interpreting Potiphar's dream of seven lean cows and seven fat cows and of abundant and withered wheat. Joseph explained the dream as a prediction that there would be seven years of abundance and then seven years of famine. Joseph advised that one-fifth of the harvest be saved each year to provide for the bad years and the famine was averted in Egypt. His brothers, however, suffering from the famine, came to Egypt to buy wheat. Joseph received them graciously, especially his younger brother Benjamin, and by this act of kindness they were reconciled and he invited his brothers to live in Egypt.

Joseph is a type or prefigurement of Jesus in his unjust suffering, forgiveness, redistribution of wealth, and his example of storing up treasures.

Joseph, Seint. The spouse of Mary (***Marie, Seinte***) and the celibate foster-father of ***Jesus***. The few facts that we have are from the opening chapters of Matthew and Luke. He was a simple and devout man, a craftsman, and devoted to the care of Mary and Jesus. He is a model of obedience to God in fleeing to Egypt, at the angel's direction, to avoid Herod's "slaughter of the innocents" in Bethlehem. A cult of Joseph was very slow to emerge, but eventually a large body of apocryphal information developed such as that he was ninety years of age at the birth of Jesus and had been married twice previously. The patron of workers, he became a special devotion of ordinary people.

Josephus Ebrayk. Flavius Josephus Ebraecus (c. 37-95) was a prolific Jewish historian especially interested in the Pharisees, Sadducees, and

Essenes. He wrote an autobiography as well as voluminous histories, which influential early Christians, such as ***St. Ambrose*** and St. Jerome (***Jeremie***), found illuminating about the Hebrew ***Scriptures***. ***St. John Chrysostom*** called him a "useful expounder" of the historical books of Hebrew Scripture. His reputation as a learned source of Scriptural commentary lived into and beyond the Middle Ages.

Jovinian, Jovinyan. An opponent of asceticism whose opinions, probably because they bordered on a Pelagian reliance on works over faith for salvation, were condemned in 390. A former ***monk***, he was a strong opponent of asceticism, especially its excesses, who held that a virgin is no better than a wife and that abstinence is no better than partaking of food moderately. He also argued that all sins are equal and that there is only one level of reward and punishment in the afterlife. He denied the perpetual virginity of Mary (***Marie, Seinte***).

His antagonism towards asceticism irritated St. Jerome (***Jeremie***) beyond restraint. Jerome's response, *Adversus Jovinianum*, excessive in its praise of virginity, devaluation of marriage, and distrust of women, was well received and repeatedly used as an authoritative text by Medieval anti-feminists.

Judas. Judas Iscariot, the apostle who betrayed Jesus to the Roman authorities for thirty pieces of silver and later, in an agony of remorse, committed suicide. His story is told in all four Gospels (Matt. 26; Mark 14; Luke 22; John 18). In the Middle Ages he was the egregious type of perfidy and betrayal.

Judas Machabeus, Machabee. Judas Maccabeus (d. 160 B.C.E.) led the Jewish revolt against the King of Syria (1 & 2 Mach.) He headed a band of guerillas from 167-161 B.C.E. His temporary successes allowed for a respite during which the Temple in the ruined city of Jerusalem was purified. Although he was diplomatically successful in enlisting the support of the Romans against Syrian oppression, Judas was killed in battle before support could materialize. His exploits are honored by the Festival of Lights. (See ***scripture***.)

Judicum. The Book of Judges; the seventh book of the Hebrew ***Scriptures***, it recounts the rule of the Judges and its main heroes are Gideon and Samson (***Sampson***).

Judith. The heroine of the Book of Judith. Nebuchadnezzar (***Nabugodonosor***) sent Holofernes (***Oloferne***) to put down the Jews. A famine caused the Jews to falter in their spirits and their defenses. Judith inveighed against them for their lack of steadfastness and courageously went to the Assyrian camp. By means of feminine wiles, she got Holofernes drunk and beheaded him, whereupon the Jews attacked and prevailed. The Book closes with a hymn to God by Judith celebrating the victory. Although there was debate, primarily because of poor texts, about the canonicity of the Book (it is not part of the Hebrew canon), it was included in Jerome's Vulgate and therefore in the ***Scripture*** that the Middle Ages knew.

Julian, Julyan, Seint. Although there are thirty-nine saints of this name in the Roman Martyrology, Chaucer clearly is referring to the fourth century, probably mythical, St. Julian the Hospitaller. He is associated with hospitality in the *Legenda Aurea*, the *Gesta Romanorum*, and the *South English Legendary*.

justice, justise, justice. Justice is the cardinal moral virtue that has reference to our relations with others. It is a moral habit which leads us to give to others what belongs to them or what they are entitled to, both on a material and a spiritual level. Justice is prior to rights granted by any political authority, though it took on meanings associated with legal systems, because it is founded on the inherent dignity of man as a creature of God. Justice is the virtue (***vertu***) whereby the rights and claims of others are satisfied—no more and no less.

Kenelm, Seint. St. Cenelm, an Anglo-Saxon saint, was crowned King of Mercia in 821 at the age of six by his father Cenwulf. From the *South English Legendary* (EETS 87:345-355), a notorious source of saints of doubtful canonicity, we learn that St. Cenelm was murdered in a plot by his wicked sister. Shortly before his death he had a veiled but prophetic dream that he had climbed a beautiful tree and that it was cut down by a servant while he was in it. It is reported that his soul flew to heaven in the form of a bird.

Kinges, Book of Kinges, Second Book of. The First and Second Book of Kings, as designated in Jerome's Vulgate, the Bible of the Middle Ages, are designated One and Two Samuel in the Hebrew tradition. It was probably originally one book though division into two parts makes sense. 1 Samuel (1 Kings in the Vulgate) deals with the history of Samuel and the reign of Saul; 2 Samuel (2 Kings in the Vulgate) deals with the life, reign, trials, and tribulations of King ***David***. (See ***scripture***.)

Laban. Laban, the father of Rachel (Gen. 29-31). His nephew ***Jacob*** consented to work without wages for seven years to earn the hand of ***Rachel***, Laban's youngest and most beautiful daughter. At the end of the period of indenture, Laban substituted Leah, Rachel's sister, whom Jacob failed to recognize until after marriage. Jacob then consented to stay on another seven years to win Rachel, during which Laban repeatedly abused him. Finally, Jacob and Rachel ran away taking with them the household tutelary gods. Laban pursued and caught them, but Jacob reproved Laban and promised not to harm either of his daughters. The story of Laban shows Jacob, the father of Israel, in an aspect of patience, perseverance, and determination. (See ***scripture***.)

Lady. *The* Lady is the Blessed Virgin Mary (***Marie, Seinte***), whose cult flourished in the later Middle Ages.

lamb, lomb. The innocent sacrificial animal is associated with ***Christ***, the Lamb of God (*Agnus Dei*). The symbolism is common in Scripture and the liturgy, notably in the Book of Revelation. (See ***scripture***.)

Lamek, Lameth. A descendant of Cain (Gen. 4:19-24) Lamech admits to his wives, Adah and Zillah, that he has killed a man and that if Cain (***Caym***) is avenged sevenfold, he will be avenged seventy-sevenfold. Thus, the curse on the house of Cain, the fratricide, continued. (See ***scripture***.)

Lamuel. Lemuel (Proverbs 31) was the Biblical king of Massa. He urges kings not to drink wine because they might forget the laws. A model of moderation, Lemuel delivers an unconscionably long homily for kings on the importance of not drinking and the benefits that a good wife brings. (See ***scripture***.)

Laudes. Literally "praises", Lauds was an early morning Church service usually recited after Matins. It is one of the earliest ritual "offices", based on antiphons and three characteristic psalms which begin "Laudate". Often mixed with Matins, it was required of the clergy though sometimes only maintained in a formal way by monks. The office of sunrise, it greets the new day, celebrating God's creation and reflecting the Resurrection. (See ***monk***.)

Lazar. The poor man in the parable of Dives and Lazarus, not the brother of Martha and Mary. Lazarus had little but crumbs from Dives' table during his lifetime. After death, Dives calls on God to allow the saved Lazarus to bring him water to ease the suffering of his damnation, but God refuses and explains that Dives has his rewards on earth and Lazarus is getting his now (Luke 16:19-31).

Lazarus. The brother of Martha and Mary (John 11:5-53). All three were friends of Jesus. At the request of Martha and Mary Jesus raised Lazarus from the dead after four days in the tomb, though both later complained to Jesus that Lazarus would not have died in the first place if Jesus had been there. Jesus demonstrates in this miracle His compassion and His power to reverse death. This miracle caused particular unease, therefore anger, among the chief priests and Pharisees. (See ***scripture***.)

lecherie, leccherie, lecchery(e), lecherye. One of the seven deadly sins (***deedly synnes***), lust or "luxurie" is one of the "tavern sins" so easily used by preachers, honest and fraudulent, in their admonitory homilies to the common folk. Lechery covers improper, that is to say almost all, sexual behavior both in thought and action including adultery, fornication, even sexual intercourse in marriage without the proper motive, and impure thoughts or desires. It encompassed any lewdness or sexual offense, but especially a habitual disposition in those directions. Its evil lies in that it is an inclination of the flesh that should be controlled by the will. Official prohibitions were frequent, but toleration and forgiveness seems to have been the order of the day.

legende. A saint's life or a collection of saints' lives or, later, any pious story with a didactic purpose. Legends were read on public occasions and were often the readings, along with Scripture, at monasteries during meals. They provided a happy source of practical example for preachers and included many highly fantastic or conjectural tales, like those of ***St. Kenelm*** or ***Hugh of Lincoln***, as well as more authentic narratives.

lent(e). The forty-day penitential season preceding Easter, characterized by prayer, fasting, and voluntary self-denial. In the fifth century, Pope St. Leo claimed that Lent was of apostolic origin. In the Middle Ages there were diverse practices to observe Lent, but ***fasting***, except on Sundays, and various degrees of ***abstinence*** were universal. The period of forty days probably was based on Christ's forty days in the wilderness (Matt. 4:1-11; Mark 1:12,13; Luke 4:1-13). In any case, the theme of Lent was preparation for the great mysteries of ***Redemption***: the Crucifixion and Resurrection of Christ.

Leonard, Seint. Little is known of the life of St. Leonard (sixth century). He, like many other revered early saints, declined worldly honors and entered a monastery. Devotion to St. Leonard, for whatever reason, gained impetus in the eleventh century for his reputed patronage of captives, women in childbirth, those possessed by a devil, and diseased men and animals. Considered a healer and liberator, he was often pictured holding chains.

licenciat. A licentiate was formal permission or authorization by the ***bishop*** or his representative to preach, hear confessions, or administer other sacraments within a designated district. Such permission was particularly necessary for itinerant friars. Secular clergy, those who did ordinary parish work, were automatically "licentiate" for the diocese in which they toiled. For others, qualifications had to be presented and formally approved by episcopal authorities.

Lollere. The Cistercian monk Henry Crumpe first applied this name at a public lecture in Oxford in 1382 to the heretical followers of John Wyclif (1324-1384), who had become numerous in the later fourteenth century. England had been relatively free of ***heresy***, but in the social and economic upheavals of the mid-fourteenth century, the Lollards (or Lollars) found favor with those with who were disillusioned with clerical power, wealth, and arrogance. Lollards attacked traditional authority and hierarchies, favoring a return to their own vision of a more primitive version of Christianity. Not only anti-clerical, they argued that insofar as sacraments had legitimacy, they depended upon the worthiness of the clergy—and they saw the clergy as largely corrupt. This led them to challenge the whole sacramental system as well as devotional practices such as pilgrimages, and to see the Bible, rather than the Bible supported by the traditions of the Church, as the supreme rule of faith. Wyclif began a translation of the Bible, completed by his followers, that made the whole of the New Testament available in English by the end of the fourteenth century. He was convicted of heresy at the London Synod of 1382 and his rejection of indulgences (***pardoun***) was repudiated by the Council of Constance in 1415. Occasionally modern critics have argued, inconclusively and not very persuasively, that Chaucer was a Lollard.

Looth. Lot, the nephew of ***Abraham*** (Gen. 18, 19). Lot accompanied Abraham to Egypt and they settled near Bethel. Because they prospered and their pastures became overcrowded, they had a dispute and decided to divide the land. Abraham gave Lot first choice; he selected fertile land near the River Jordan and resided in Sodom. Two unidentified angels arrived at the house of Lot. The Sodomites wanted to have their way with them, but Lot resisted and offered his daughters instead. The Sodomites refused; the angels struck them blind, and revealed themselves in the morning as heavenly messengers. They commanded Lot, his wife, and daughters to flee and not look back at the evil city of Sodom, which was being destroyed. Lot's wife looked back and was turned to a pillar of salt.

Towards the end of the narrative (Gen. 19:30-38), Lot's daughters got him drunk, slept with him, and became impregnated so that he would have progeny. Lot led a turbulent and mysterious life, often on the edge of divine law. (See ***scripture***.)

love. The somewhat secular word "love" became a common term for the theological virtue of charity (***charitee***). As such it is an infused virtue and involves God's love for us and our love for God in Himself and as manifested in self, others, and the divinely created world. (See ***vertu***.)

Loy, Seint. St. Eligius (c. 588-659) lived according to a strict Irish monastic rule, which he introduced to a convent of 300 virgins in Paris.

The founder of several monasteries, he had a public reputation for arranging the ransom of prisoners and alms for the poor. After his public and monastic exertions he became a priest and Bishop of Noyon-Tournai. He is the patron of goldsmiths, metal workers, and blacksmiths. After his death, his relics (***relikes***) were popular objects of special veneration.

Luc. St. Luke the Evangelist, physician and author of the third canonical Gospel, was not a Jew. Nevertheless, learned in Greek, he had a profound knowledge of the Septuagint, the Greek translation of the Hebrew Scriptures. Thoroughly familiar with the Greek world, he was a close associate of St. Paul (and probably of other Apostles) and wrote the Acts of the Apostles. His Gospel, based on written sources (he had probably read ***Matthew*** and ***Mark***), is full of parables and miracles and often, like Acts, seems designed for a Gentile audience. Thus Luke, like ***St. Paul***, was influential in disseminating the Christian revelation beyond the Jews. (See ***scripture***.)

Lucifer. Lucifer, meaning shining or light-bearing, is identified by St. Jerome (***Jeremie***) as the leader of the fallen angels who rebelled against God. Therefore, he is Satan (***Sathan***), the Devil himself, not some minor demon. His name apparently recalls the brilliance of his glory before his rebellion.

lust. The most common name for the deadly sin of ***lechery*** or ***luxurie***. However, of the various terms for illicit sexual behavior in thought or action, lust is the one that most often emphasizes the underlying disposition towards a disorder in the appetites that makes it a capital or root sin. (See ***deedly synnes***.)

luxurie. Unlawful sexual desire, thought or action; synonymous with lechery (***lecherie***) and ***lust***. It is one of the seven deadly sins as a disposition that allows the inclinations of the flesh to overwhelm the will. (See ***deedly synnes***.)

lymytour. A friar (***frere***), so-called because his begging, preaching, and power to administer the sacraments, especially ***Penance***, was limited to a particular pre-approved geographical jurisdiction. As friars wandered, they always needed to gain the official sanction of the hierarchy of the district within which they wished to operate. In practice, the system was riddled with abuses and some unscrupulous friars roamed at will.

Machabee. The Book of Maccabees, included in the Vulgate, recounts the exploits of ***Judas Machabeus*** the Jewish warrior, patriot, and diplomat. (See ***scripture***.)

Magdalene, Magdelene, Magdeleyne. There is confusion about whether St. Mary Magdalene was one or three persons: in one manifestation she was the woman frequently associated with Jesus who ministered to Him (Luke 8:2-3), had seven devils cast out (Mark 16:9), was at the foot of the Cross (Luke 23:49), saw Christ laid in His tomb (Matt. 27:61; Mark 15:47), and was the first recorded witness of the Resurrection (Mark 16:1-8; Luke 24:1-10).

The Greek Fathers distinguished three Marys Magdalene: the one described above, the sinner of Luke 7:36-50, and the sister of Martha and Lazarus (Luke 10:38-42). The Latin Fathers saw all three as one and the same. In any case, her reputation in the Middle Ages was primarily as the reformed sinner who demonstrates genuine penitence and shows Christ's forgiveness.

Mahoun, Makomete. Mohammed (c. 570-630), the founder of Islam. Upon a call from the angel Gabriel in 612, Mohammed became a prophet of Allah. Although little is known of his personal life, he incited anger and persecution, and fled from Mecca to Medina in 622 (the Hegira), the beginning of the Mohammedan or Islamic era. Mohammed united various tribes and returned triumphant to Mecca.

Islam was a movement of militant evangelism. In 732 Charles Martel preserved Rome by defeating the Muslims at Tours, but by the twelfth century they were in control of Western Asia, North Africa, and Spain. Even though they were defeated by the Mongol Turks in the thirteenth century, the Turks accepted Islam. From a Christian perspective Mohammedans were violent and godless pagans, the barbaric vipers of the Holy Land and the enemies of the Crusades.

Mardochee. In the Book of Esther (***Ester***), Mordecai is Esther's uncle, who adopts her upon the death of her father. When she was chosen by

Assuer, King of Persia, Mordecai stayed with her and advised her. He discovered a plot to kill the king and told Esther, who told the king. He also informed Esther cf a plan by Aman to kill all the Jews in the kingdom in a year. He was rewarded by Assuer.

Mordecai instituted the feast of Purim to celebrate the thwarting of Aman by Esther. (See ***scripture***.)

mariage, marriage, maryage. The ***sacrament*** of Matrimony. The word applies both to the event and the state—a permanent union of a man and woman. Monogamy was required, but even serial marriages were sometimes called into question because, after all, what would you do at the time of the resurrection of the body after the Second Coming of Christ? The institution is used metaphorically to figure forth the relationship between Christ and his Church; nuns (***nonne***) were sometimes called "brides of Christ". On a less austere level, the anti-feminists persistently vilified marriages as the scourge of man, and St. Jerome (***Jeremie***) and other ascetics asserted that virginity was a higher, more perfect state than marriage, citing the example of Christ's virginity.

MARIE, MARYE, SEINTE. The Blessed Virgin Mary; the mother of Jesus. There are frequent references to the Blessed Virgin Mary in Chaucer, usually as some variant of "St. Mary" in mild oaths and asseverations. This usage is not blasphemous but rather a sign of how seriously the cult of Mary was taken in the later Middle Ages. The Blessed Virgin Mary has been honored among Christians since antiquity, but devotion to her especially flourished during the Middle Ages. The development of this devotion closely coincided with the development of Christology. That is, as Christians came to a deeper understanding of who Jesus is, this understanding was reflected in an ever-deepening devotion to his mother. Conversely, Marian devotion has brought with it a deeper understanding of ***Christ*** (especially His Incarnation). In terms of medieval piety, ***St. Bernard*** (1090-1153) expressed this intimate link between devotion to Mary and devotion to Christ:

> Do not forget to make all that you decide to offer pass through Mary, so that grace, by returning to its Author, may take the same path that it took in its descent. ("Sermon on the Nativity" V)

Likewise, the English monk Aelred (1109-1166), the so-called "Bernard of the North", preached:

> If ... we wish to ascend to the place from which he descended, that is, to the Father of heaven, let us begin our ascent from the son of Mary, that is, from the humanity of Christ. ("Sermon on the Nativity of the Blessed Virgin Mary")

By the time Christian tradition had been expressed in the canonical collection of writings that came to be known as the New Testament, the singularity of Jesus' birth was highlighted by an emphasis on His mother's virginity in conceiving Him. (See the first chapters of both Matthew and Luke.) After several centuries of lively controversy over the relationship between Jesus' humanity and his divinity, the doctrine of the Incarnation (God made flesh) was encapsulated in Mary's title, *Theotokos* ("Mother of God"). The appropriateness of this honorific was hotly debated but finally resolved in the ecumenical Council of Ephesus (A.D. 431). Its significance for Christology—that Christ was not two persons, one divine and one human, but one person with two natures—flowered in the popular imagination with the realization that the mother of Christ was also mother of all Christians. For by Baptism (***Baptesme***), each Christian is incorporated into the body of Christ, and the mother of the head (Jesus) must also be mother of the whole body (the Church). The New Testament had already signaled this intimate union: Paul on the road to Damascus heard Jesus ask him, "Saul, Saul, why do you persecute me?" (Acts 26:14), and in his letters reflected on this identification of Jesus with his persecuted members. Matthew's Gospel reflects this identification as the criterion of final judgment: "As long as you did this for the least of my brothers, you did it for me", Jesus will say at the end of time (25:40). John's Gospel also announces the identity of the mother of Jesus with the mother of the disciple (understood as *every* disciple, every Christian) as Jesus' final bequest at the end of His life (John 19:26). Finally, the Book of Revelation (***Apocalips***) depicts the Church symbolically as the Woman in terms that were applied to Mary (Rev. 12).

More than a mere symbol or metaphor, however, Mary's motherhood infused Christian piety with a sense of her personal intimacy and concern for each of her spiritual children. More than mother of the Church, she had come to be seen, as early as the second century, as the representative or advocate for all humanity: Recapitulating this long tradition, Thomas Aquinas, in the thirteenth century, wrote that her consent to become the mother of Jesus was an affirmation uttered "in place of the whole of human nature" (ST III.30.1). In so doing, she became the new Eve, as writers as early as Irenaeus (second century), Epiphanius (c. 315-403), and Jerome (347-420) described her. By this obedient consent, she reversed the first Eve's disobedient consent to sin (by eating forbidden fruit). As the first Eve thus condemned her children (all humanity) to death, Mary as the new Eve reversed this condemnation by bringing forth Christ, the source of eternal life for all her children. Medieval Latin emblematized this reversal by pairing Eve's name ("EVA") with the first word of the angel Gabriel's greeting to Mary ("AVE") in Luke 1:28 (see below). For instance, the hymn, "Ave Maris Stella" plays on this reversal:

Sumens illud "AVE" Gabrielis ore ...
Mutans Hevae nomen.
(Taking Gabriel's "AVE" ["Hail!"] ...
Reversing Eva's name.)

Coupled with the belief in the communion of saints, this belief in the motherly concern of Mary for all sinners naturally gave rise to the pious habit of seeking Mary's intercessory prayers as one approached the "throne of grace" (Hebrews 4:16). Just as a vassal of a great king might seek the intercession of a kindly queen mother, or a chivalrous knight would approach his lady for a favor, the Christian entered God's presence in the company of Mary and the other saints. Worship in the strict sense was reserved for God alone, but honor, veneration, and devotion given to exemplary Christians like Mary and other saints amplified, rather than diminished, God's glory, just as an earthly ruler's glory was amplified by the splendor of his courtiers.

Sometimes, though, this distinction between worship and veneration was blurred in practice. In the "Prioress's Tale", the Prioress, a refined but intellectually unsophisticated nun, reflects her simple devotion to Mary, which is emphasized in her own Prologue, and her Tale itself is a "miracle of the Virgin". The tale concerns a young student who is murdered by "brutal Jews" as he walks through the ghetto singing the hymn "Alma Redemptoris Mater". (Curiously, the Jews had been expelled from England before the end of the thirteenth century.) The hymn honors Mary, appropriately, as the mother of the Redeemer. Of course, the boy, ignorant of Latin, has learned the hymn by rote, much like the Prioress' own simple and unsophisticated devotion. One who knows his Latin well would see that the very center of this invocation of Mary is the "Redeemer", Jesus; similarly one well schooled in Medieval piety would recognize that to call on Mary was to call on Jesus. But this young boy is not well schooled, and his devotion to Mary may cross the line between authentic veneration and superstition.

The simplicity of the Prioress in this Tale, especially in her childlike devotion to Mary (as she speaks of herself in her Prologue), may appear to be a dangerous and mindless innocence in this tale of Jewish brutality and equally brutal Christian retribution—the Jews are slaughtered indiscriminately. Although the moral understanding and sensibility of the Prioress may be questioned, the theology concerning Mary is orthodox. (The Prioress's religious education would have been rather superficial at the convent outside of London where she was educated, and the portrait of her in the "General Prologue" suggests a superficial sense of self as a courtly lady rather than a religious—apparently unconscious.) It seems that Chaucer is subtly satirizing both the Prioress and the student of the story for their misplaced devotion, while recognizing the warmth and power of authentic Marian spirituality.

Devotion to Mary took the popular form of the Rosary (see ***bedes***), a concatenation of short prayers drawn from the Gospels ("Our Father" and "Hail Mary"). Since these short prayers could be easily memorized, the Rosary allowed even the illiterate to echo the daily prayers of monks and nuns--a daily sequence of seven services consisting primarily of the psalms and other passages from the Bible. (See ***monk***.)

Outside the monastery, those individuals who could afford the expense of a prayer book, hand copied and painstakingly illustrated ("illuminated"), could follow these monastic liturgies in their private or family devotions by reading along in their "Hours" (as these books were called in Chaucer's time). Those who could not afford such a book, or who could not read one in any case, could emulate the daily prayer of the monks by substituting, for the 150 psalms, 150 recitations of the "Hail Mary" to sanctify the day and night. In the spiritual company of Mary, the pious Christian "pondered within his heart" the great things that God had done on his behalf (Luke 2:19). By the fifteenth century, these "great things", the so-called "mysteries" of the Rosary, were arranged into three groups: the joyful, the sorrowful, and the glorious, commemorating respectively the life, death, and resurrection of Jesus, but also the parallel joys, sorrows, and final hoped-for glory in the Christian's own life.

The very structure of the "Hail Mary" reflected this spirituality: the prayer begins by repeating the joyful, praise-filled salutations addressed to Mary by the angel Gabriel and Mary's cousin Elizabeth, inspired by the Holy Spirit:

Hail [Mary], full of grace,
the Lord is with you (Luke 1:28).
Blessed are you among women,
and blessed is the fruit of your womb (Luke 1:42),
JESUS CHRISTUS

AMEN.

At the climax of the prayer, Jesus is worshipped. Thus, the inspiration of the Holy Spirit and the example of God's word through an angel lead the sinner toward Jesus through Mary. Jesus is at the heart of the prayer, as the incarnate God-man. Here one stops to worship, but as the ***pilgrimage*** of life continues through time toward death, the pilgrim goes forth in the company of the mother of the Church and the mother of all the living, through death to final glory.

Not only the day but also the year was seen as a symbolic pilgrimage. At each season, Mary is remembered. Her birth is celebrated in September. As the expectant mother, her figure comes to dominate the winter Advent season. The Christmas season celebrates her virgin-motherhood: from the birth of Jesus, through her showing Him to the Gentiles (Epiphany), to the beginning of His public life with His first miracle at her request at Cana (John 2:1-12). In early spring and Passiontide, she stands with Jesus at the foot of the Cross. May is her month as she gathers with the Apostles in the upper room to watch and pray for Pentecost (Acts 1). In mid-August, she is laid to rest, only to be rapt into glory (the feast of the Dormition or Assumption). Her life, then, parallels both the life of Jesus and the spiritual life of every Christian, of whom she is both mother and model.

These daily and annual spiritual pilgrimages paralleled physical pilgrimages to shrines, cathedrals, and other holy places dedicated to the Blessed Virgin. In England it was customary to have a chapel in each cathedral called the "Lady Chapel" dedicated to Mary. Both in England and on the continent, entire cathedrals and monasteries were also dedicated to her. Indeed, by the Middle Ages, this pious custom of dedicating holy places to Mary had a long pedigree: shortly after the Council of Ephesus (see above), Pope Sixtus III erected a basilica in Rome to honor Mary as the Mother of God—the oldest church in the West in her honor, now called St. Mary Major because of its primacy.

FURTHER READING: O.R. Vassall-Phillips, *The Mother of Christ: or, The Blessed Virgin Mary in Catholic Tradition, Theology, and Devotion* (London: Burns, Oates and Washbourne, 1936); Giovanni Miegge, *The Virgin Mary: The Roman* Catholic *Marian Doctrine*, tr. John A. Mackay (Philadelphia: Westminster Press, 1955); Michael O'Carroll, C.S.Sp., *Theotokos: A Theological Encyclopedia of the Blessed Virgin Mary* (Wilmington, Del.: M. Glazier, c. 1982); Jaroslav Pelikan, *Mary Through the Centuries: Her Place in the History of Culture* (New Haven: Yale University Press,1996).

Marie Egipcien, Seint. St. Mary the Egyptian (c. 344-421) was a prostitute for seventeen years. On a pilgrimage to Jerusalem, presumably to ply her trade, she tried several times to enter the Church of the Holy Sepulchre to venerate the relic (***relike***) of the True Cross. Mysteriously unable to enter, she weepingly asked a statue of Mary (***Marie, Seinte***) for guidance and was told to cross the River Jordan. That same evening, when she reached the Jordan, she was baptized in a church devoted to ***John the Baptist*** and wandered eastward into the desert where she lived a solitary life on herbs for forty-seven years.

She encountered the monk and priest Zossimus, who asked her to meet him the following year on Holy Thursday. She is reported then to have walked on water and then received Communion. Zossimus returned a year later to find her corpse: she had died on the very night she had first received the Eucharist. On the whole, her life seems more bizarre than exemplary.

Mark. St. Mark the Evangelist, the author of the second canonical Gospel of the New Testament. His Gospel concentrates on Jesus' ministry in Galilee, and although Mark was a Jew, his Gospel seems more designed for a Gentile audience. Although not an apostle, he was an associate of St. Paul named John Mark and mentioned in the Acts of the Apostles (Acts 12:12) and two of Paul's Epistles (Col. 4:10 and 2 Tim. 4:11). According to common belief, he went to Alexandria to evangelize and was martyred there in the reign of Nero. His remains were traditionally said to have been moved to Venice. (See ***scripture***.)

martir(e), martyr. A martyr suffers death, and usually torture, for steadfast profession of and fidelity to his or her faith. Most of the early saints were martyrs, for martyrdom ensured salvation. Martyr comes from the Greek word for one who testifies to a fact. If the fact was Christ's revelation, that put one in a particularly vulnerable position under the Roman Empire, where failure to accept the "state gods" was grounds for execution.

Although the heroism of a martyr's testimony was highly honored, it was forbidden to seek out martyrdom. It was, however, still rather easy to come by in the early centuries of Christianity. The extended sense in which the term was frequently used is clear in Chaucer's and the Church's identification of ***St. Thomas*** a Becket as a martyr.

Martyn, Seint. St. Martin of Tours (c. 316-400) was a Roman soldier but attracted to Christianity. A famous legend says that upon meeting a beggar he divided a cloak with him; the cloak preserved as a relic (***relike***). After he had spent ten years in eremitic solitude, a group of monks gathered around him. He under took evangelistic journeys in pagan Gaul where numerous local legends about him survive.

Although consecrated Bishop of Tours, he withdrew and founded a great monastery. His cult was very popular in the Middle Ages and many stories of his holiness, generosity, and wonder-working circulated. He was buried at Tours in a grand sarcophagus which, over the years, has been repeatedly desecrated.

Mathew. St. Matthew the Evangelist, author of the first canonical Gospel of the New Testament probably in Antioch in the last quarter of the first century. He was called to be an Apostle from his booth as a tax collector, an odious occupation, as an example of Christ's reaching out even to the outcasts of Jewish society. His Gospel apparently relies on Mark, but it would be odd for an eyewitness, someone who was himself an Apostle, to use such a source. Eusebius, our major fourth-century source for early Church history reports that Matthew worked among Gentiles in remote areas late in his life. (See ***scripture***.)

matrimoigne, matrimoyne. The married state, the bond of marriage, or the sacramental event of ***marriage***. (See ***sacrement***.)

MESSE. The Mass is the central, official, and public worship service of the whole Catholic Church, celebrated daily. Early on it became a daily requirement for the clergy. For others, attendance at Mass was required on Sunday and feast days. At Jesus' Last Supper when he commanded his Apostles, "Do this in remembrance of me" (1 Corinthians 11:23-25), he provided Mass to be celebrated in all times and places (Malachi 1:11) until he returns (1 Corinthians 11:26). The next day on the cross, Jesus offered once for all (Hebrews 9:12 & 26; 10:12-14) his death as a sacrifice for the sins of the world (John 1:29). In offering Mass, the Apostles, their successors (bishops), and the priests ordained by them repeat the celebration of that sacrifice. At each Mass, Christ's bloody, sacrificial death is made present in an unbloody way under the sacramental signs of bread and wine. (See ***sacrement***.)

By the thirteenth century, the doctrine of transubstantiation expressed in precise philosophical language the relationship between the bread and wine on the one hand, and the body and blood of Jesus on the other: "the whole substance of the bread is changed into the whole substance of Christ's body, and the whole substance of the wine into the whole substance of Christ's blood. Hence this is not a formal, but a substantial conversion; nor is it a kind of natural movement: but, with a name of its own, it can be called 'transubstantiation'" (Aquinas, ST III.75.4).

To see the relationship between the singular historical event, Jesus' crucifixion, and the on-going worship of the Mass, it is helpful to think of three types of temporality:

1. In historical time, events are unique and unrepeatable occurrences. Thus, Jesus died once and for all at a particular time (c. 30 A.D.) and place (Calvary).
2. In sacramental time, a unique historical event can be re-presented (made present again and again) in different times and places through the power of a sacrament to effect what it signifies. Thus, in every Mass the unique death of Jesus is re-presented in such a way that the worshippers at that Mass (say, at Canterbury in 1390) are virtually present at Calvary in 30 A.D. The many Masses celebrated in various times and places all flow from and are united in the single event of Jesus' sacrifice on the cross.
3. If time is a limitation, eternity is the absence of that limitation, such that all reality is present all at once in an endless, dimensionless "now". Thus, Jesus eternally offers himself to God the Father on behalf of sinners in a never-ending sacrifice.

This single and unique event (the sacrifice of Jesus) thus occurs on three levels: once and for all historically, in various times and places sacramentally, and forever eternally. The Mass mediates these three levels by uniting worshippers both with the historical death of Jesus and the eternal sacrifice in heaven.

There was great variety in the forms of the ritual in the Middle Ages ranging from simple masses to solemn pontifical masses celebrated by the ***Pope*** or a ***bishop***. The precise elements and sequence of events were not entirely settled by the fourteenth century, but the essential, and some traditional, elements are clear. The Mass had two parts: the Mass of the Catechumens and the Mass of the Faithful. These two parts corresponded to the modern Liturgy of the Word and Liturgy of the Eucharist. The first refers to the practice of dismissing catechumens (new converts who were preparing for Baptism) after the sermon, since only the baptized could receive other sacraments (such as the Eucharist). Known in ancient times as the *disciplina arcana*, secrecy surrounding the sacraments was at least superficially similar to the secrecy surrounding the rites of pagan cults. In addition to the intrinsic desire to screen what was most sacred and to follow the Gospel injunction of not giving to "dogs what is holy" or "casting pearls before swine" (Matt. 7:6), there was also the extrinsic and pragmatic motivation of avoiding detection in times of persecution. Those already baptized and remaining in full communion with the Church by embracing its doctrine, authority, and moral way of life—the "faithful"—stayed to complete the Mass. The Mass of the Catechumens, which everyone attended, was much like a synagogue service and probably modeled on it; it consisted primarily of readings from Scripture, hymns or psalms, prayers, and on Sundays, at least, a sermon.

The principal subparts of the Mass of the Faithful were the Offertory (presentation of offerings), the Canon (including the Consecration, the recitation of Jesus' words at the Last Supper instituting the Eucharist—"This is my body. This is the chalice of my blood, of the new and eternal covenant, which will be shed for you and for many, for the forgiveness of sins"), and the Communion (sacrificial meal under the forms of bread and wine). By the end of the thirteenth century it had become customary to conclude the service with a reading of the beginning of St. John's Gospel.

Long before the fourteenth century, the Mass was celebrated in Latin—even after it was no longer anyones first language—often as a solo performance by a priest with his back toward the congregation *versus Deum* ("toward God") at an altar flush against a wall of the church or chapel. With little or no participation by anyone other than the priest, an entire Mass could be celebrated—perhaps even reverently—in twenty minutes. In fact several Masses could be celebrated simultaneously in the same church building. One story (unverified) has it that a certain nobleman arranged for several priests to begin Mass in succession, a few minutes apart—like the singing of the round, "Row, Row, Row Your Boat"—so that individual members of his hunting party could drop in at whim to find a Mass somewhere in the church just reaching what many considered the most graced moment, the elevation of the Host at the Consecration. Thus, his hunting party could be on its way to the day's activities with only the minimal delay occasioned by piety. Whatever the truth of that story may be, it illustrates a common attitude, not unlike that of some contemporary Californians with their drive-in funeral parlors.

FURTHER READING: Josef Andreas Jungmann, *The Mass of the Roman Rite, Its Origins and Development (Missarum Solemnia)*, tr. Francis A. Brunner, rev. Charles K. Riepe (New York: Benziger Bros., 1959); Edward J. Kilmartin, *Christian Liturgy: Theology and Practice* (Kansas City: Sheed and Ward, 1988); Robert Cabie, *History of the Mass*, tr. Lawrence J. Johnson (Portland, OR: Oregon Catholic Press, 1992).

Michias. The minor prophet Micah, the sixth among the minor prophets (their books were short) and a contemporary of the major prophet (their books were long) Isaiah. Micah prophesied the impending destruction of Samaria and then Judah, warning that God requires strict observance of the Mosaic Law, not just sacrifices. The people repented and God withdrew his threat of the destruction of Zion. The Book of Micah includes Messianic prophecies of a period of peace following the triumph of Israel over her enemies. Thus Micah delivers a standard prophetic diet of indictment for moral failures, prediction of impending doom, and a concluding Messianic hope. (See ***scripture***.)

misericorde. A corporal work of mercy (from the Latin *misericordia*); pity, or compassion, was a Christian duty especially toward the needy and persecuted.

MONK. The word derives from the Latin *monachus*, though the English form "munuc" developed by the tenth century. It identifies someone who withdraws from the secular world into seclusion in order to sanctify his own life and to benefit the rest of the Christian community by a life of religious contemplation and prayer. All Christians are bound by Christ's precepts commanding what is necessary for charity and forbidding what is incompatible with charity. His counsels of poverty, chastity, and obedience, however, seek to remove obstacles to charity for those who are called to this simpler path. Monks are those who follow these counsels by joining a religious community, more or less contemplative, with vows of poverty, chastity, and obedience, and a commitment to follow the rule of his particular order, such as the ***rule*** of St. Benedict (***Benedight***) or the rule of St. Augustine (***Augustyn***).

The monastic tradition had its beginnings in the retreat of individuals to remote or isolated locations. This tradition of individual withdrawal, "anchorites" or "hermits", was especially common in the early Eastern Church, though it existed in the West and took a particularly ascetic form in Ireland. The father of Christian monasticism is generally considered to be ***St. Antony*** (third century), who, although he lived most of his life as a hermit, for a while gathered around him a group of like-minded associates. From such beginnings, monks called cenobites, to distinguish them from hermits, gradually came to live in loose associations and then in more formally organized communities under the governance of an abbot or prior, a superior elected by the monks themselves except in the case of a charismatic founder. United by the idea of *contemptus mundi*, contempt or rejection of the things of this world, monks were committed to the twin goals of *orare et laborare*—to pray and to work—free from the distractions and temptations of ordinary life.

In addition to private devotions and reading, their prayers included communal recitation of the "divine office" or "hours", in keeping with the biblical injunction to "pray without ceasing" (1 Thess. 5:17) throughout the day and night. Although their daily tasks inevitably interrupted their prayers, monks approximated constant prayer by frequent prayer. The natural rhythms of the day and night became a natural counterpoint to this prayer: sunset signals a time for resting and reflecting, for giving thanks and commending one's dear ones to the Lord, as the end of day suggests the end of earthly life. Waking or keeping vigil through a long night occasions leisurely meditation. With the morning comes joy (Psalm 30:5) and praise for a new day and new life. As the sun climbs to the zenith, midmorning and noon are natural moments for brief pauses for prayer, as is the mid-afternoon counterpart to midmorning, when the sun is halfway between zenith and horizon. Thus, daily communal prayer in the monasteries spanned the day and night suspended from these eight pylons: Vespers (literally, "evening prayers") at sundown, Compline ("completed") at bedtime, Matins ("morrow") during the night, Lauds ("praises") at dawn, Prime ("first hour") at sunrise, Tierce ("third hour") at midmorning, Sext ("sixth hour"; cf. Spanish "siesta") at noon, and finally Nones ("ninth hour") at mid-afternoon.

Although anchorites persisted in the East and to a lesser extent in the West, the institution of monasticism became associated with these communities who gathered together to work and pray. Members were usually not priests so as to avoid the danger of pride, though some were ordained in order to perform the liturgy for the community, and in fact the proportion of priests increased over the years. All monks took four vows: poverty, which prohibited the ownership of personal property; chastity, which proscribed marriage and sexual activity of any kind; obedience, to Church authority in general and to the abbot in particular; and stability, a commitment to live and work within the physical confines of the monastery and its arable fields. An exception was made for ***outriders***, monks designated to attend to the external affairs of the monastery usually having to do with the sale of the goods they produced or purchase of what they could not make for themselves. The physical community where the monks lived, the monastery, often became known as a cloister (*cloistre*), although strictly speaking the cloister was the courtyard within the monastery especially devoted to contemplation and the recitation of prayers.

In addition, monks living in communities committed themselves to abide by a specific ***rule***, a set of prescriptions about every aspect of their life, work, diet, demeanor, responsibilities, and spiritual exercises. The two most common rules were those of St. Augustine (***Augustyn***) and St. Benedict (***Benedight***), although some local variations developed. Other rules sprang up from time to time, but the Church discouraged the proliferation of monastic orders to preserve some consistency and perhaps to facilitate some degree of control by the hierarchy. In any case, Augustinian and Benedictine foundations flourished in the Middle Ages and the Benedictines were so successful that they became almost synonymous with monasticism.

Comparable communities of women, ***nonnes***, grew up at about the same time, usually associated with the Augustinian or Benedictine rule. Their foundations were also called monasteries and the rules were, if anything, more strictly defined and circumspect especially with regard to chastity. The application of the term "convent" (***covent***) for a community of women was a much later development; indeed communities of men were often also called convents in the Middle Ages.

The history of monasticism often seems to be a pattern of decline and reform, the most notable reform being that of the Benedictines by ***St. Bernard*** of Clairvaux, who called them back to a stricter adherence to the rule of St. Benedict. The very industry of the monks, occasioned by their commitment to their ideal of work and the generosity of wealthy patrons, sometimes resulted in an unseemly accumulation of capital. Thus in the fourteenth century, the monk became an easy and frequent butt of satire for a paradoxical disposition towards greed and self-indulgence of all sorts. Although they were obvious targets, on the principle that "the corruption of the best is the worst", there is little doubt that the worldly monk of Chaucer's "General Prologue" and the unscrupulous monk of the "Summoner's Tale" were not unfamiliar figures. (See ***Augustyns***.)

FURTHER READING: Eleanor Shipley Duckett, *The Gateway to the Middle Ages: Monasticism* (Ann Arbor, MI: University of Michigan Press, 1961); David Knowles, *Christian Monasticism* (New York: McGraw-Hill, 1969); Ludovicus Milis, *Angelic Monks and Earthly Men: Monasticism and its Meaning to Medieval Society* (Rochester, NY: Boydell Press, 1992).

Moyses. The central Biblical patriarch and guide of God's chosen people. Exposed as child because of a decree that all the Jewish children born into Egyptian captivity be killed, Moses was found and raised by Pharaoh's daughter, but as a young adult, out of pity for his people, he killed an Egyptian taskmaster and fled (Exodus 2:1-22). After forty years as a shepherd he was called by God to represent his people against the increasingly oppressive Egyptians (Exodus 2:23-12:33). Despite his feelings of unworthiness and incapacity, he spoke for his people and with the assistance of God, Who brought ten plagues on the Egyptians, ultimately he led his people into freedom. Thus he was a leader and liberator, but his greatest role will be as lawgiver and prophet when he received the Ten Commandments from God on Mt. Sinai, thereby becoming priest and mediator for the Jews. (Exodus 12:34ff). (See *scripture*.)

Nabugodonosor. Nebuchadnezzar II (esp. Daniel 1-5) reigned over the Babylonian Empire from about 605 to 563 B.C. Although he was a moderate by contemporary standards, the Book of Daniel narrates the punishment of his pride. Having captured Judah and taken ***Daniel*** and three companions prisoner, Nebuchadnezzar, when his magicians and astrologers failed, called upon Daniel, who had already been of valuable service, to interpret his dreams. The most important was an immense image of gold, silver, and bronze, with legs of iron, and feet of iron and clay, which was destroyed by a huge rock that grew into a mountain. Daniel interpreted this as a succession of kingdoms (Nebuchadnezzar's is the gold) ultimately issuing in the fall of secular power and the triumph of the kingdom of God. Daniel was honored, but when Daniel's companions refused to worship an idol, they were put in a fire (the three young men in the fiery furnace), but were neither killed nor consumed. As a result, the king honored Daniel's God.

Daniel was also able to read the mysterious "handwriting on the wall" inscribed by a disembodied hand. It meant, according to Daniel, that Nebuchadnezzar had been judged by God and found deficient and that his kingdom would be taken by the Medes and Persians. That very night Darius conquered the kingdom. As Nebuchadnezzar is a symbol of pride, Daniel is a symbol of the wisdom of holiness. (See ***scripture***.)

Nazarenus. See ***Jhesu Nazarenus Rex Judeorum***. St. Jerome (***Jeremie***) construed Nazarene to mean "flourishing".

necessite(e). In a philosophical sense, necessity is fate or predestination. It has religious significance because it comes into conflict with free will and thereby becomes involved in the voluminous Medieval controversies about the apparent contradictions between freedom, fate, God's foreknowledge of human events, and Divine Providence (***purveiaunce***). (See ***fate***, ***foreknowynge***, ***freedom***.)

Nichanore. Nicanor was a Syrian general in the Books of Maccabees (1 Macc. 3; 2 Macc. 8). He attacked the Jews, confidently expecting to sell them into slavery. Some Jews, disheartened, deserted, but ***Judas Machabeus*** rallied the rest with religious and patriotic rhetoric and they routed Nicanor in the first major defeat of Antiochus. This Nicanor is not to be confused with Alexander the Great's general of the same name.

Nicholas, Seint. As a young man St. Nicholas (fourth century) made a pilgrimage to the Holy Land and shortly after became Bishop of Myra. Imprisoned under the Emperor Diocletian, he was released under Constantine the Great. An exceptionally large number of miracles were attributed to him. He is the saint who has become associated with Christmas as Santa Claus by means of a number of highly conjectural explanations.

Noe. When God found men corrupt and immoral beyond correction particularly because of their intermarriage with Canaanite women, he sent the flood to wipe out most of his own creation (Gen. 5-9). But God found Noah and his wife and his three sons, Shem, Ham, and Japheth, worth saving and a means to give another chance to the human race. Noah was commanded to build a large boat (ark) to precise specifications and to load on board his family and two of every living thing, so that a new beginning would be possible. The rains came and the ark floated for forty days, finally coming to rest on top Mt. Ararat. As soon as they were on dry land, Noah offered a sacrifice, in strict adherence to the Mosaic Law, of seven pairs of clean and two pairs of unclean animals. (One imagines that what they were we will never know.)

The Christian Scriptures contain many references to Noah as a just and obedient man. Noah was a familiar character for Medieval audiences in the mystery (cycle) plays of the fourteenth and fifteenth centuries. "Noah's Flood", in the Chester Cycle, represents Noah in his traditional holiness and obedience and his wife as a lighthearted version of the recalcitrant wife so dear to the hearts of the anti-feminists. (See ***scripture***.)

nonne. A nun. From very early in Church history there were communities of women devoted to a life of religious perfection, virgins dedicated to God's work. The variety of kinds of communities was great: virgins who took solemn vows authorized by a *bishop*, deaconesses in the service of the Church, the wives or widows of men who had taken Holy Orders, sometimes just a loose association of high-minded women with no formal vows.

Gradually these communities became organized into more formal religious establishments. St. Jerome (***Jeremie***), for example, wrote to the nuns of St. Paula in Bethlehem and they adopted the ***rule*** of St. Augustine (***Augustyn***), thus becoming more like the monastic or mendicant communities of men. Indeed, many male orders developed female counterparts like the Dominicans and, most notably, the Second Order of St. Francis (the Poor Clares). Among the mendicant orders there was the huge difference that women were required to live in ***cloister***, to live entirely enclosed. Orders of nuns took on the education of young women, the care of the sick, and the performance of other corporal works of mercy. As was the case with many priests, their education was not all that might have been desired.

Note, Seinte. St. Neot is an obscure saint largely lost in the mists of ninth century England, though there is a town St. Neot's near Cambridge. He is said to have risen during the night to pray, apparently with uncommon regularity and endurance since this practice was in itself so common as to be hardly noteworthy. He is also thought to have had some role in Alfred's (supposed) founding of Cambridge University.

novys. A "beginner", specifically a recent entrant into a religious ***order***. A novice was past the stage of postulancy, or formal commitment, and had been officially accepted into the order. His or her status, however, was probationary and characteristically accompanied by a series of tests and a strict regimen to establish the firmness of his or her vocation to the religious life. Although a novice was considered a true "regular", or member of the order, and was able to claim "benefit of clergy", *i.e.*, the right to be under the jurisdiction of the ecclesiastical courts (***Court Cristien***), he or she had not yet taken formal vows and had to engage in a period of study, self-examination, and spiritual exercises before the profession of sacred vows and permanent admission to the community. A comparable probationary period was required for entrants into other religious vocations requiring vows, but the term was applied most commonly to probationers in monastic (***monk***) or mendicant (***frere***) orders or their female counterparts.

Nowelis flood. The forty-day flood from which Noah (*Noe*) and his family are permitted by God to save themselves in order to assay a new beginning for mankind. There is an analogue of this flood in the Assyrian epic Gilgamesh.

Nynyve(e). Nineveh, the ancient capital of Syria, was the hotbed of sin and corruption to which Jonah (***Jonas***) was sent. Although Jonah, ultimately to his chagrin, saved the city by his prophetic admonitions, it was renowned as a place of riches, power, and moral dissolution.

obedience. The virtue of submission to legitimate authority, especially God. Such, of course, is the duty of all Christians, and it is emphasized in famous examples like the story of Noah (*Noe*). However, obedience took on a specific meaning for the religious orders, for whom it was one of the three universal vows, along with poverty and chastity, and included to submission to the authority of the superior of the religious community, *e.g.* ***abbot***, ***abbess***, ***prioresse***.

offertorie. The part of the Mass (***messe***) in which the offerings of the congregation, usually in solemn procession, are presented prior to the beginning of the canon, the central part of the Mass. It is a gesture of humility and submission to God. More liturgically, it refers to the rite in which the bread and wine are presented as an offering to God before the Consecration in which their substance is transformed into the body and blood of ***Christ*** and, by extension to the prayers or chants associated with the rite.

offryng(e). The ***Offertory*** of the Mass. It could be associated with a gift to the Church, but more basically it indicated the processional of offering or the gifts offered.

Olde Testament. The Old Testament is the designation of the Hebrew ***Scriptures*** (plus other pre-Christian works) used by Christians as early as Origen (c. 185-232) and Clement of Alexandria (d. 215). It is distinguished from the New Testament, the Christian Scriptures, which deal with the ministry of Christ, His passion, death, and Resurrection, and with the early spread of Christianity. Over time Old Testament came to imply the Old

Law and the New Testament implied that the Old Law had been superseded by a new, and higher, dispensation.

Oloferne, Olofernus. Holofernes was Nebuchadnezzar's (***Nabogodonosor***) military commander who led a ferocious campaign against the Israelites, described in the Book of Judith. Enchanted by Judith's beauty, he was vulnerable to her and she beheaded him in his drunkenness. The story captivated the Middle Ages perhaps because it had everything—evil, blood, gore, beauty, revenge, and moral edification.

ordre. Any one of the religious communities of ***monks***, friars (***frere***), ***canons***, or nuns (***nonne***) who live according to a common *rule* such as the Benedictine or Augustinian. The religious orders were a source of power and satisfaction to the Medieval Church in their piety, zeal, good works, and example of the ideal of the Christian life, but they were also, too frequently a source of shame and satire when members deviated from the ideals they professed. Certainly, they provided a treasury of scholars and saints, though also not a few rogues.

In another sense, order can refer to the "holy orders" taken by the clergy. There was a variety of specified functions in the liturgy and administration of the Church, though some minor orders developed into simply names for preparatory stages in preparation for the priesthood. There were three or four "major" (or "sacred") orders: ***bishop***, priest (***prest***), deacon (***dekne***), and subdeacon (***subdekne***) (there was some dispute as to whether the bishop and priest were of one order rather than two). The terms "bishop", "priest", and "deacon" are Anglicized forms of New Testament Greek words: *episkopos* (literally, "overseer"), *presbyteros* (literally, "elder"), and *diakonos* (literally, "servant" or "waiter").

The bishops collectively form a "college" which carries on the mission given by Christ to the original Twelve Apostles, namely, to teach, govern, and sanctify the faithful in Christ's name. As the original Apostles died, their place in the "Apostolic College" was taken by successors (see Acts 1), who in turn were replaced by others, in an unbroken line down to the current bishops. This is what is meant by "apostolic succession". Like the original Apostles, the bishops teach by handing on the teaching of Christ; they govern by calling the faithful to an evangelical way of life, in imitation of Christ; and they sanctify by celebrating the ***sacraments*** instituted by Christ to make His grace available in every age. In this three-fold office of teaching, governing, and sanctifying they carry on the mission of Jesus, who is called "Christ" ("Anointed One") because he unites in His person the three types of anointing in ancient Israel, namely, prophetic (teachers), kingly (governors), and hieratic (sanctifiers).

Priests are vicars (***vicaire***) of the local bishop, who delegates to them authority to preach and celebrate all of the sacraments (except Holy Orders itself—only a bishop can ordain clergy).

Deacons assist bishops and priests, especially in works of charity. They are sometimes authorized to preach, to baptize, and to officiate at weddings and funerals, but not to celebrate Mass, hear confessions, or administer other sacraments. In Chaucer's time, deacons remained deacons only a short while and typically went on to be ordained as priests. Similarly, candidates for the priesthood passed through the transitional rank of subdeacon (***subdekne***).

There were also four minor orders, typically held by men preparing for the priesthood: porter, lector, exorcist, and acolyte. In contradistinction to major orders—which were conferred by the sacrament of Holy Orders, instituted by Christ—minor orders had neither the effect (an "indelible character"—a permanent change in the very being of the recipient which makes the recipient resemble Christ more closely and calls forth special graces appropriate to the duties entailed by the sacrament) nor the sacramental power of major orders. That is, although a recipient of minor orders was a cleric, he had no inherent authority to do anything a layman could not do, at least in principle. In practice, of course, a cleric in minor orders had duties not given to the laity, such as reading from Scripture in official public worship.

ordres four. The four mendicant orders of friars (***frere***): Dominicans, Franciscans, Carmelites, and Augustinians (***Augustyns***).

Oreb. The Biblical Mr. Horeb (Mt. Sinai), the mountain of God, where Elijah (***Elye***), after fasting and meditation, speaks with God and is given his prophetic mission and where Moses (***Moyses***) is given the Ten Commandments.

oriso(u)n. A prayer or the act of praying.

o(o)th. A solemn promise, usually with the invocation of God or a saint (***seint***), or relics (***relike***), or other holy objects, to perform some laudable action, to keep an agreement, or otherwise to be true to one's word. An oath is a serious matter, not to be undertaken lightly, because it calls upon God to witness the commitment to the intention, and failure to carry through could be sinful. However, oath also has a less ponderous imposition as a curse or expletive. In either case it should not be confused with a ***vow***.

outridere. A member of a monastic order permitted to "ride out" away from the monastery presumably on the necessary business of the order, like the monk in the *Canterbury Tales*. Such offices would be essential in connection with the business and financial affairs entailed by the productivity of the monastic commitment to work. The most common outrider was the "cellarer" (***celerer***), the provisioner for the monastery, who would have to engage in frequent business with the outside world such as bartering for necessary items or overseeing the monastery's proprietary grange. One can imagine that the temptations encountered in such a role would be greater than those faced by the general run of ***monks***.

palmeres. Religious pilgrims, originally to the Holy Land, so-called because of the practice of returning from the pilgrimage carrying a palm leaf as a sign of the devotional journey they had undertaken. Later the term was applied to pilgrims who visited other religious shrines such as St. James Compostela and Canterbury. Palmers not only included simply devout laymen but also itinerant monks whose vocation was to travel from shrine to shrine, penitents who were enjoined by their confessor to undertake a ***pilgrimage***, and some folks who just wanted a jolly few days in the countryside away from their humdrum daily lives.

Parabels of Salomon, Parablis. A collection of wise sayings (Proverbs 10:1-22:16) attributed to Solomon (***Salomon***), the revered judge and lawgiver. There is little distinctive about these sayings, which give moral and moralistic advice on how to live the good life, except perhaps in their emphasis on the importance of *prudence*. They are not parables in the more familiar sense of narratives with a moral significance.

paradis, paradys, paradys. From the Greek word for "pleasure ground", paradise could refer to either end of the human experience: the Garden of Eden, where Adam and Eve lived before the Fall, and heaven, the location of our ***salvation***. In the former sense, it is a melancholy reminder of the tribulations of man's post-lapsarian state. In the latter sense, it was the ultimate goal and reward of the saved. Augustine's view of paradise (*City of God*: 22), conveyed to the Middle Ages by Pope Gregory I, was central and primary: the joy of paradise was the experience of the Beatific Vision, a direct experience of the goal and greatest good of our existence. St. Bonaventure emphasized love as the prime ingredient, Aquinas intellect. In any case, it was seen as a real place, where the resurrection of the body would occur and the saved would live in everlasting bliss in communion with God.

PARDO(U)N. There were two religious senses of the word in common use in the Middle Ages. 1. Pardon was the forgiveness of sins accomplished by virtue of the priest's granting of *absolution* in *Confession*, the *sacrament* of *Penance*; 2. More commonly in the Middle Ages a "pardoun" referred to indulgences. An indulgence is not to be confused with the absolution from sin in the sacrament of Penance. After absolution, there remained the necessity for *satisfaction*, the expiation for forgiven sins which still needed to be accomplished in this life or in ***purgatory***. An indulgence was an extra-sacramental remission in whole (a plenary indulgence) or in part (a partial indulgence) of the temporal punishment still due to sin after sacramental forgiveness. The Church as a spiritual network (the "Communion of Saints") is helped by the prayers and merits of each member but hurt by the sins of each member, no matter how secret. This is obvious in the case of social acts: a single act of kindness can have repercussions into the far distant future, as the beneficiary of that act may become a little more kind to someone else, who in turn benefits a third person, and so on. So, too, with hurtful acts. This solidarity in good and evil is less obvious with interior acts (thoughts, prayers, attitudes) but no less real, given the spiritual interconnectedness of all the faithful, both living and dead.

The practice of granting indulgences apparently originated in eleventh century France, ordinarily as a prerogative of the ***bishop***, and as late as the thirteenth century it was seen as a kind of concession to the weakness of some of the faithful. During the succeeding centuries the doctrine suffered from much confusion and perhaps more abuse. Problems arose both from venal clerical abuse (at all levels) and from misunderstandings of the difference between absolution and indulgences. Attempts were made to restrict the prerogative to the Pope, but the power to grant indulgences was gradually extended back again to bishops and sometimes assumed by them without papal authority. The practice was restrained by the Fourth Lateran Council (1215). Later other prelates and eventually, under special licenses, archdeacons (***erchedeken***) and ***pardoners***, neither of whom even had to be clerics, were permitted to grant indulgences. The fact that there was often a price, papal or otherwise, for indulgences was the source of much of the abuse (or at least the suspicion of abuse.) Pope John XXII's levy for the indulgence for the Canterbury pilgrimage of 1320 was so high that it put the Christchurch foundation in debt for the year.

Indulgences were commonly granted on the occasion of major religious feasts or events such as the consecration of a church, the canonization of a saint, or the celebration of a jubilee year. The price could be high and the motive could be suspect: in 1350, Clement VI offered a plenary indulgence for ***pilgrimage*** to the Holy Land, but later compromised at least appearances by granting the indulgence to anyone who contributed the cost of such a trip. On a humbler scale, indulgences were granted for the performance of some specified action such as making an ordinary pilgrimage, venerating a relic (***relike***), undertaking some penitential regimen, or even for almsgiving.

Controversy abounded. Both Clement V (r. 1305-1314) and the Council of Constance (1415) reminded the faithful that indulgences did not, as some mistakenly or disingenuously claimed, grant absolution for unforgiven sins or provide a license to sin in the future (a kind of absolution in advance.) In 1392, Pope Boniface IX noted that many claims, erroneous or spurious, had been made for indulgences which were not authorized by Church doctrine. Nevertheless, because of the proliferation of licensees, such as pardoners, and because of the (sometimes intentional) confusion of almsgiving with bribes, abuses persisted and continued to give scandal to the doctrine.

The late fourteenth-century reformer-heretic John Wyclif completely denied the efficacy of indulgences of any kind, but his contentions were specifically repudiated by the Council of Constance (1414). The real abuses of indulgences, however, escalated in the fifteenth century to become a major issue in the Reformation. The Council of Trent (1545-1563) upheld the theological propriety of indulgences provided that the recipient was in a state of grace (free from sin), had the intention to receive the indulgence, and performed prescribed works. The damage to the Church, however, was already done.

FURTHER READING: Henry C. Lea, *A History of Auricular Confession and Indulgences in the Latin Church* (New York: Greenwood Press, 1968); John G. Deedy, *Retrospect: The Origins of Catholic Beliefs and Practices*, esp. pp. 95-110 (Chicago: Thomas More Press, 1990); Richard P. McBrien, *Catholicism* (San Francisco: HarperSan Francisco, 1994).

pardone(e)r. Pardoners were usually clerics hired by religious foundations, or sometimes freelancers, who traveled around under diocesan license offering indulgences (***pardoun***). Since the granting of indulgences was usually associated with almsgiving, whatever else was entailed, pardoners were in a uniquely tempting situation. Despite repeated denunciation by Popes and prelates, the office was frequently abused, although it had a sound and sanctioned theological basis. Whatever the dangers to the spiritual well-being of the faithful, the institution gave rise, among the pardoners, to some of the virtuoso preachers of the age.

parson, perso(u)n(e). A parish priest, member of the secular clergy. His duty was to care for the spiritual needs of his parish by saying Mass (***messe***) and administering the ***sacraments***. There was great difficulty in recruiting a literate pastoral clergy in the fourteenth century, with the better educated clerics entering orders such as the Franciscans or, especially, the Dominicans. They were, however, mostly held in high regard by the ordinary people because of their generally modest styles of life and their demonstrated dedication in ministering to the sick and dying during the plague years in the late 1340s and early 1370s.

parvys. Parvis. The portico of a Church. More broadly it was the enclosed area or court in front of a church or public building, a location where clients consulted lawyers at specific columns. In Chaucer's experience the most noteworthy such location would have been at St. Paul's Cathedral in London where "sergeants of the law" were inducted as full-fledged lawyers.

passio(u)n, passyoun. Something to be suffered or endured, most specifically associated with the sufferings and death of ***Christ***: scourging, crowning with thorns, crucifixion—all part of the suffering undertaken by Christ as part of the redemptive act. The Passion of Christ became a focus of meditation to encourage sorrow for sin, which had caused these horrendous and undeserved sufferings of Jesus. Direct attention to the Passion was slow to develop until the writings of ***St. Bernard*** of Clairvaux (1090-1153) and St. Francis of Assisi (1181-1226). Then many facets of the Passion became elements in the mystery (cycle) plays of the fourteenth and fifteenth centuries making the Passion a prominent and visible fact of life in the later Middle Ages.

On a moral philosophical level, a passion is a human desire or inclination, usually sexual, towards sin or evil. It is a lower order of desire, a manifestation of the weakness of the ***flesh*** to be controlled by the reason and will.

pater-noster. The Lord's Prayer presented in the Gospels (Matt. 6:9-15; Luke 11:2-4). Because it was scriptural, the prayer that Jesus taught us to say, it became a prominent part of Christian devotion. It became part of the ritual of Baptism and was incorporated into the Mass, immediately after the canon, by Pope St. Gregory. The term was also applied to beads or a string of beads (*bedes*) on each of which a "pater noster" was said.

Pathmos. Patmos, a small volcanic island in the Aegean off the coast of Asia Minor where St. John was supposedly exiled and wrote the Book of Revelation.

patriarkes. Scripturally the historical and theological founders of the Jewish tradition, especially ***Abraham***, ***Isaac***, and ***Jacob***, but also other distinguished figures such as Noah (*Noe*) and, particularly, Moses (*Moyses*).

Chaucer's use of the term, however, is restricted to the derived designation of an office in the religious hierarchy of the church. Patriarchs were the highest ranking dignitaries after the Pope, bishops of special dignity, honor, or geographical extent. The title was more commonly used in the Eastern Church (schismatic, heretical, or faithful), though Rome was a patriarchate.

Paul, Poul, Paulus (Seint). Except for the Roman consul mentioned passingly in ***Boece***, St. Paul. Born in Tarsus to a Roman citizen father, he was Saul at circumcision and Paul as a Roman citizen. Paul was an animated opponent of Christianity until his vision of Christ on the road to Damascus. Thereupon he began his evangelistic career (45-57) as apostle to the Gentiles. In Asia Minor he concentrated on the cities, though his tireless travels took him to most of the civilized world. Much of his life is recounted in the Acts of the Apostles. He was imprisoned at Caesarea, sent to Rome, and executed towards the end of the reign of Nero.

Paul was long associated with ***St. Mark*** and St. Luke (*Luc*), the Evangelists, and, though he was not a personal associate of ***Christ***, because of his actions and achievements he is sometimes honored as the "thirteenth Apostle", especially for evangelism to the Gentiles. Some consider him the second founder of Christianity especially because of the influence he exerted on *St. Augustine* and, thereby, the subsequent history of the Church. He is especially notable for his theology of grace, his emphasis on the "justifying" power of grace, his concentration on the idea of Redemption, his defense of the sacraments and the ecclesiastical system, and his asceticism (sometimes bordering on anti-feminism.) A prolific writer, he is the author of thirteen canonical ***Espistles***.

payen(s). An individual or group ignorant of the true God and the Christian revelation. Pagans lack Baptism (***Baptesme***), though the term does not ordinarily include Jews. More often the term refers to Moslems or other distant folks. They are often assumed to be given to violent and barbaric behavior, especially the violent persecution of the Christian Church. In view of this attitude, it is odd to note the history of attempts at forced conversion recounted in the *Song of Roland* and many other narratives. One supposes they were just being coerced for their own good.

payne, peyne. The negative effects of sin are two-fold: guilt ("culpe") and punishment ("peyne"). Sinners can and should cooperate with the redemption won by Christ by their own sufferings and mortifications. ***St. Paul*** wrote, "Now I rejoice in my sufferings for your sake, and in my flesh I complete what is lacking in Christ's afflictions for the sake of his body, that is, the church..." (Col. 1:24). Accordingly, the penance of an individual can contribute to the spiritual welfare of the whole church. Even when a sinner repents and restores his good standing with God and the human community, guilt may be forgiven, but there are still lingering after-effects. Sin brings with it its own punishment in the form of other natural adverse consequences: the ungrateful no longer enjoy benefactions; the hostile are alienated; the intemperate are plagued by disease, weariness or addiction; the dishonest are no longer trusted; the slothful are frustrated by failure and sadness.

These lingering effects are called collectively "the temporal punishment for sin" (as distinct from eternal punishment, *i.e.*, ***hell***). Temporal punishment can be remedied by self-imposed disciplines (mortifications). For instance, the gluttonous can overcome some of the effects of intemperance by a healthier regimen of diet and exercise. Of course, the more one is given over to gluttony, the harder and more punitive will such remediation appear.

A prayer, a pilgrimage, an alms, or other pious labor, performed with the right intention—that is, in a spirit of repentance and reparation for sin—can reduce or eliminate temporal punishment due to sin. Moreover, by the Communion of Saints, such pious work under some circumstances may be applied to the temporal punishment due to another, even someone deceased, provided that he died repentant, in the state of grace. That is, the deceased is forgiven, and thus freed from guilt, but not yet holy, for the lingering effects of sin remain. Yet God is utterly holy, and nothing unclean may enter his divine presence. Hence, the deceased must be fully sanctified in order to enter heaven. This state of final purification of repentant sinners in or after death is called ***purgatory***. It can be aided and accelerated by the pious acts of others, and, first and foremost, by the infinite merits of Jesus' life, death, and resurrection. Such aid is called an "indulgence". The Church, with the authority conferred by Jesus, determines the particular conditions for gaining an indulgence, either partial or plenary remission of temporal punishment.

penance, penaunce. The ***sacrament*** of Penance in which, by contrition, ***confession***, and ***satisfaction***, one is absolved of sins committed. On a more specific level, it is the contrition or sorrow required within the sacrament or the regimen of punishment or satisfaction prescribed by the priest for satisfaction.

penitauncer. A priest empowered to hear confessions and grant ***absolution***, *i.e.*, administer the ***sacrament*** of ***Penance.***

penitence. The disposition towards and practice of repentance including contrition or sorrow for sin and a purpose to amend one's life. It includes such elements as prayer, ***fasting***, bodily hardship, or spiritual exercises undergone as ***satisfaction*** for sin.

penitent, penytent. One who has the disposition of ***penitence*** and undertakes the behavior proper to it.

Peter, Petre, Seint. Born Simon, Peter was given his new name by Christ because it means rock, and Peter would be the rock-like foundation of the Church. Although married, he was attracted by John the Baptist's preaching of penance and called by Jesus to be an Apostle with his brother Andrew. Increasingly in the Gospels Peter emerges from among the other apostles as first among equals. With ***James*** and ***John*** he witnessed the Transfiguration of Christ (Matt. 16:28-17:3; Mark 9:1-13; Luke 9:27-36) and Christ's agony in the Garden of Gethsemane (Matt. 26:36-46; Mark 14:32-42; Luke 22:39-46). Christ gives him, metaphorically, "the keys to the kingdom" (Matt. 16:13-20; Mark 8:27-30; Luke 9:18-21); this is the basis upon which the Church traced the authority of the Papacy back to Peter. After the Resurrection he received special attention and commissions (John 21:20-23). His early apostolic works are described in the Acts of the Apostles. He is believed to have been in Rome during the latter part of his life, hence the designation of him, and subsequent Popes, as the Bishop of Rome. According to the accounts of Origen and Tertullian (***Tertulan***) in the second century, St. Peter was crucified upside down because he felt unworthy to be martyred in the same way that Christ was executed.

Pharao, Pharoo. The monarchs of Egypt, especially the one who asks ***Joseph*** for the interpretation of his dreams (Genesis 40) and the one whom Moses (***Moyses***) deals with in securing the liberation of the Jews from captivity (Exodus 1-15).

Pharisen. Pharisees, a political-religious faction prominent from about the third century B.C. They were radical separatists, extreme Jewish purists, sometimes called "the Jewish Puritans" in their zeal to distance themselves from the heathen and the unorthodox. Though vigorous supporters of conservative ideals and defenders of tradition, their methods and influence were democratic rather than priestly. They are, however, frequently cited by Christ as example of intransigence and pride.

(ad) Philipenses (secundo). St. Paul's Epistle to the Philippians, written from prison. Chapter 2 especially counsels humility, but that is not the point of Chaucer's Parson's reference to the honored name of Christ.

Philistiens. The Philistines inhabited the maritime plain of Biblical Palestine. Perennial antagonists of the Jews, they were repulsed by Saul (1 Sam.) and more decisively defeated by David (2 Sam.). Perhaps their most famous conflict, however, was the one with Samson (***Sampson***) (Judges

13-16). They are, for the Middle Ages, a symbol of barbarism and lack of civility as a result of their constant enmity towards the Jews.

Phitonissa. After Saul forbade the consulting of ghosts and spirits, he himself visited Phitonissa, the witch of Endor, who conjured up Samuel for him. Samuel reproved Saul for this behavior and predicted his defeat and death. Then, when routed by the Philistines, Saul fell on his sword (1 Chron. 10:13; 1 Samuel 28:7)

Piers, Peter Alfonce. Petrus Alphonsus, a Spanish Jew, was converted to Christianity in 1106. He was a formidable controversialist, who wrote a six volume "dialogue" between Christian and a Jew and, more importantly for the fourteenth century, *Disciplina Clericalis*, a moral treatise loosely based on Arabic wisdom but adapted to orthodox Christianity.

Pilates (voys). Pontius Pilate was the Roman Procurator of Judea, the local governor, during the public ministry of ***Christ***. He is the type of the worldly, political man who would have preferred to acquit Jesus, but yielded to Jewish pressure because he thought his public position was threatened (Luke 23). Pilate was a popular character in the Medieval mystery (cycle) plays and was usually portrayed with a loud, ranting voice.

PILGRIMAGE, PILGRYMAGE. A journey undertaken individually or, more often, in a group to a religious site or shrine, ordinarily the repository of a relic (***relike***). Generally, the purposes of a pilgrimage were to venerate the relic, to ask for divine help, or to fulfill some religious obligation.

The earliest pilgrimages were to the Holy Land to visit sites associated with the birth, life, ***passion***, and death of ***Christ***. As early as the second century, certainly by the fourth, the Holy Land attracted relatively large numbers of the faithful. An arduous and dangerous journey, the pilgrimage was often undertaken with armed guards, especially after Jerusalem fell to the Moslems. However, the fascination of the Holy Land remained great, and of course it abounded in relics, real and manufactured. It might be argued that the Crusades were an extreme form of pilgrimage, or an attempt to make the world safe for pilgrimages.

Next in importance after the Holy Land as a destination for pilgrimage was Rome with its many associations with early saints and martyrs and its identification as the seat of Christianity. Rome offered certain advantages to the pilgrim because it did not require a dangerous sea journey or exposure to hostile Moslems. As pilgrimages grew in popularity in the early Middle Ages, many destinations emerged. Early in the ninth century, after the "discovery" of the remains of ***St. James*** the Apostle in Compostela in northeastern Spain, an area recently recovered from the Moors, the shrine of St. James Compostela became the third most popular destination after the Holy Land and Rome.

To Englishmen, however, especially those of the more ordinary sort, even northern Spain was a daunting journey, and so pilgrimage sites began to emerge in Britain. By far the most famous and popular was ***Canterbury***, the place where ***Thomas*** a Becket, the Archbishop of Canterbury, had been murdered on December 29, 1170. Immediately upon his death and persistently thereafter, an abundance of miracles were attributed to him. In a remarkably short time even for the Medieval Church, Thomas was canonized by Pope Alexander III on February 23, 1173. Pilgrimages to Canterbury surged, although they decreased in number within about ten years, perhaps because they were often made to coincide with the saint's day, which for St. Thomas meant the depth of winter, perhaps because of the proliferation of other shrines throughout England.

On July 7, 1220, however, the remains of St. Thomas were "translated", moved to a more appropriately elegant tomb. A great resurgence of interest in Canterbury followed, maybe because of the more auspicious time of year for traveling, but probably more because of a general increase in the popularity of pilgrimages, which peaked shortly after the mid-thirteenth century. Canterbury, however, remained popular at all times of year through the fourteenth century and beyond. This popularity was sustained by the excellent road (the ancient Roman road called Watling Street) from London, the population center, to Dover, with Canterbury along the way. Contemporary records indicate that the pilgrimage to Canterbury was attractive to all levels of English society. Because of the good road, the journey to Canterbury could be accomplished in a brisk two days or a more leisurely three and a half days.

The purposes of pilgrimages, on which pilgrims characteristically brought offerings of value suited to their social station, to leave at the site, were various. A pilgrimage was sometimes enjoined by a confessor on a penitent in expiation for an especially public or serious sin. It was sometimes undertaken by penitents out of their own personal sense of regret for a life of sin. Most often, it was a simple act of piety, with the hope of gaining some spiritual, or material, favor by the intercession of the venerated saint. Frequently, it included the reception of an indulgence (***pardoun***). Indeed in 1320, the hundredth anniversary of the translation of St. Thomas, Pope John XXII granted a plenary (full) indulgence to anyone who made the Canterbury pilgrimage that year. Finally, by the fourteenth century the Christian fellowship that had generally been a part of pilgrimages had tended to take on an even more convivial atmosphere, making a pilgrimage an attractive outing. Pilgrimages were an opportunity to travel, a break from routine, but it would be cynical to say that they had become wandering festivals. The fourteenth century found it easier than we do to combine piety and picnic.

From the very beginning, however, pilgrimages were subject to criticism from serious churchmen as occasions of sin either because of frivolity or excess or the tendency of human beings to loosen up when out of town. From St. Jerome (***Jeremie***; c. 340-420) to Thomas a Kempis (c. 1380-1471) serious warnings were issued by the clergy. Notable, though perhaps especially severe, was the tirade of John Bromyard, a ferocious fourteenth century Dominican: "There are some who keep their pilgrimage not for God but for the devil. They who sin more freely when away from home or who go on pilgrimage to succeed in inordinate and foolish love—those who spend their time on the road in evil and uncharitable conversation may indeed say peregrinamur a Domino—they make their pilgrimage away from God to the devil." (*Summa Praedicantium*) We may be reminded of some of Chaucer's pilgrims, but we should also remember that Bromyard tended to be vigorously against everything. (See ***palmers***.)

FURTHER READING: Donald John Hall, *English Mediaeval Pilgrimage* (London: Routledge & K. Paul, 1965); Jonathan Sumption, *Pilgrimage: An Image of Medieval Religion* (Totowa, NJ: Rowman and Littlefield, 1975); Howard Loxton, *Pilgrimage to Canterbury* (Newton Abbot, Eng.: David and Charles, 1978); Diana Webb, *Pilgrims and Pilgrimage in the Medieval West* (New York: St. Martin's Press, 1999).

pistel. See ***epistel***.

POPE. The Pope, the Bishop of Rome, is the supreme leader of the Church and, according to the Church, traces his authority back, by apostolic succession, to St. Peter. By the ***sacrament*** of Holy Orders, the Pope is consecrated as one bishop among many. His primacy is derived not from that sacrament but from the ancient status of Rome and its first bishop Peter. Although papal infallibility in matters of faith was not defined as an article of faith until the First Vatican Council (1870), the spiritual authority of the Pope had been accepted at least since the second century and certainly was firmly established by the fourteenth. Controversies tended rather to be over the degree of secular authority wielded by the Pope, particular irregularities surrounding the election of specific Popes by the college of ***cardinals***, and the corruption of some incumbents. The titles of the Pope suggest his unquestioned power: Pontifex Maximus ("the great bridge-builder", *i.e.*, between heaven and earth) and Servus Servorum Dei ("the servant of the servants of God", an ironic truth that could be countenanced only by a legitimate autocrat).

The Pope appointed bishops, issued decrees deciding questions of the faith and discipline, and acted as a final arbiter in all spiritual matters. When, from time to time, a Pope argued the right to appoint the Holy Roman Emperor, secular authorities objected and even devout Christians like Dante were of the party that held that the Pope was supreme only in spiritual matters. In the first half of the fourteenth century, the English monk and scholar William of Ockham challenged the secular authority of the Pope, most notably in *Compendium Errorum Joannae XXII* (*Compendium of Errors of John XXII*) and *Quaestiones Octo de Auctoritate Summi Pontificis* (*Eight Questions concerning the Authority of the Supreme Pontiff*). In 1328 he was cited at the papal court of John XXII (r. 1316-1334), but fled to the protection of Ludwig of Bavaria.

That John XXII was in residence at Avignon rather than Rome is a sign of the disarray of the Papacy in the fourteenth century. Clement V (r. 1305-1314), a Frenchman, had resided in the recently acquired city of Avignon from 1309, but in 1348 the disputed Clement VI (r. 1342-1352) officially moved the seat of the Papacy to Avignon and thus began the "Great Schism" (or "Babylonian Captivity") with rival popes reigning in Avignon and Rome. The rift was not closed until the Council of Constance officially restored the Papacy to Rome in 1417. The dispute significantly diminished the practical power of the Papacy during most of the fourteenth century.

FURTHER READING: Friedrich Gontard, *The Chair of Peter: A History of the Papacy*, tr. A.J. and E.F. Peeler (New York: Holt, Rinehart and Winston, 1964); Geoffrey Barraclough, *The Mediaeval Papacy* (London: Thames and Hudson, 1968); Walter Ullmann, *A Short History of the Papacy in the Middle Ages* (London: Methuen, 1974); Michael J. Walsh, *The Papacy* (London: Weidenfeld and Nicolson, 1997).

possessioners. Those ***monks*** and secular priests (***prest***) who lived on the income from land or endowment. This was not the situation of all monks and secular priests and certainly not the case with friars (***frere***), who lived as mendicants with ownership of property forbidden even to their religious orders. It was particularly the situation of the so-called ***chantry*** priests, who lived in communities singing Masses (***messe***), for a fee, for the rich and famous; their fees often eventuated in an endowment.

poverte(e). The state incurred by the renunciation of ownership of the things of this world. Although this word had the secular meaning with which academics through the ages have been familiar, more narrowly it is one of the three vows taken by ***monks***, friars (***frere***), and ***canons regular***. While monks generated their subsistence by their commitment to work and canons regular by being ***chantry*** priests or being attached to a university, the vow of poverty was most extreme for friars, whose orders could not even hold wealth in common. Indeed, many friars set out on their preaching missions with the confidence of faith but without a penny. Abuses, however, were sufficiently common that self-indulgent monks and friars were frequent targets of satire in the fourteenth century.

prechour(e)s. Anyone who proclaimed the word of God in public for an audience, but especially friars (***frere***) who thereby earned their bread; most notably the Dominicans, the Order of Preachers (or ***Freres Prechours***), who were renowned for their scholarship and oratory. Preaching had developed into a high form of rhetorical art by the fourteenth century, including elaborate formulas for the citation of a Biblical text, explication of the text, and poignant and entertaining exempla exhorting the laity to reform their lives. Traveling preachers needed a license from the bishop or his representative to speak in a particular episcopal or monastic jurisdiction.

PREDESTINACIOUN. The foreordination by God of specific human events, up to and including the salvation or damnation of individuals. The doctrine of predestination appears to contradict the attribution of free will to human agents required for moral praise or blame.

St. Thomas Aquinas wrote, "Now there is no distinction between what flows from free will, and what is of predestination; as there is no distinction between what flows from a secondary cause and from a first cause" (ST.I.23.5). This is a key statement about God's Providence (***purveaunce***): every detail, every particular being, action, or event in the cosmos is sustained and governed by God's action as the first cause. God may make use of secondary (instrumental) causes, which have a causality and therefore a responsibility of their own, but they remain radically dependent on God's activity. Consider an everyday example: a small child may help her father change the oil in the family car. The father is perfectly capable of doing everything himself, but the child wants to help. So the father gives her small tasks, such as handing him a particular wrench or rinsing the oil pan's plug in a cleaning fluid, all under his watchful eye and careful direction. The child adds nothing to the process but superfluous activity, and yet in some real sense she is a secondary cause.

In fourteenth-century England, Thomas ***Bradwardin***, an Oxford professor who became Archbishop of Canterbury in 1349, gave a rise to a theological current which so emphasized predestination that the freedom of the human will was denied, if not by Bradwardin himself, by his follower John Wiclif (1324-87), whose determinism and fatalism led him to conclude that sacraments administered by a non-elect priest were invalid and that ecclesiastical or political power exercised by a non-elect official was illegitimate. Moreover, the non-elect could not own property. In the Council of Constance, Session VIII, May 4, 1415, the Church rejected as heretical Wiclif's position that the "prayer for the foreknown is of avail to no one". (See ***fate***, ***foreknowynge***, ***purveaunce***.)

FURTHER READING: See **purveaunce**.

predicacioun. A sermon or preaching. (See ***prechours***.)

prela(a)t. Strictly, the incumbents of Church hierarchical offices with specific jurisdictions, but commonly, any ecclesiastical personage of high rank or dignity within the Church and of corresponding authority. In the fourteenth century, prelates would have included the ***Pope***, and important officers surrounding the papacy: ***bishops***, ***cardinals***, ***patriarchs***, deans of cathedrals and collegiate churches, and heads of religious communities such as ***abbots***, provosts, and priors. Sometimes a cleric of eminent accomplishments could be considered a prelate even if he no longer held a specific office.

prescience. Foreknowledge, especially God's foreknowledge of what human beings will do. This was a necessary belief if God were not to be limited, but it conflicted, in the eyes of some, with the doctrine of free will. Scholastic philosophers, by placing God outside of time, removed the problematic issue of human notions of cause and effect. (See ***foreknowynge***.)

pre(e)st. Below a bishop and above a deacon, a priest was the primary minister of the Church with the power to say mass (***messe***) and administer the ***sacraments***. Ordained by the ***bishop*** of the diocese, priests owed obedience to the bishop and took a vow of celibacy. Priests may be broadly divided into two groups. The secular clergy, whose usual duties were as parish priests entrusted with the spiritual care of those in their jurisdiction, did not take a vow of poverty but were usually poor in fact. Although often not very well educated, simple parish priests were generally held in high regard by the populace because of their compassion and courage treating the sick and dying during the outbreaks of plague in the late 1340s and early 1370s.

The regular clergy were those who lived in communities according to a ***rule***, such as ***monks***, friars (***frere***), and ***canons regular***. Monks and friars did not have to be priests (***prest***) but increasingly were ordained in the fourteenth century. Their varied, often scandalous, reputations are amply documented by the satire of Chaucer and many of his contemporaries.

The word was also used for Jewish religious leaders as well since it applies to those who lead sacrifice and worship.

pride. The first of the seven deadly sins (***deedly synnes***). At its root is an excessive sense of one's own worth and prerogatives. Pride was sinful both as a disposition and as an act which put oneself above God or above one's legitimate superiors in a hierarchical world. An appropriate love of self was honored as appropriate to the dignity of a person created by God, but arrogance and excessive ambition were not only a deadly sin but perhaps even the root of all sin in the way that sin arrogates to man choices which are not properly his. The opposing virtue is humility.

prime, pryme. A short ritual office, like Terce, Sext, and Nones. At first it was called *matitutina* (*hora*); later to distinguish it from the nocturnal hours of Matins and Lauds, it became known as "Prime".

Prime is first mentioned in the rule of St. Benedict (***Benedight***), the praying of the "canonical hours" being especially a monastic practice. ***Monks*** were tending to sleep in after Lauds until Terce (about 9:00 a.m.). Prime was introduced to be said about 6:00 a.m. so that the monks would be up and working until Terce. The indication of times is rough since these "canonical hours" varied somewhat with the season. (See ***monk***.)

prioresse. The superior in a monastery for women. Sometimes the title was reserved, as opposed to ***abbess***, for superiors of freestanding convents (***covent***) that did not have an affiliation with others but operated simply under episcopal authority. The title could also be used for the second in charge after an abbess, entrusted with supervision of the ***cloister*** itself. Like abbesses, prioresses usually came from the upper classes; they were welcomed at manor houses and at great public and religious events, a circumstance which worked against their ideal of seclusion. However, bishops repeatedly forbade secular journeys and even pilgrimages in the fourteenth and fifteenth centuries.

professioun. A public declaration of faith. It came to be applied especially to the entering of a religious state of life or to the vows of poverty, chastity, and obedience (and sometimes stability) taken on such an occasion. It applied to the declarations of men and women (nuns [***nonne***], ***monks***, friars [***frere***], ***canons regular***, *etc*.), and sometimes referred to the assumption of the religious habit associated with the chosen way of life. A solemn profession was considered "perpetual", and the person could only be released from such professed vows by the bishop, and even then only with great difficulty.

prophete. An inspired and holy teacher who claims to speak on behalf of God. Prophets have become associated with foreseeing the future and predicted doom, but their role is mostly to lament and warn. The Hebrew prophets were sent by God to communicate His will. Supernaturally enlightened, they condemned current moral failings, either warned against or predicted future cataclysm, but ultimately prepared the way for the Messiah and the establishment of the renewed kingdom of God. Prophets are essentially oral messengers; the biblical books associated with them are records of their activities and counsel. The four "Greater Prophets" of the Hebrew tradition are Jeremiah, Isaiah, Daniel, and Ezekial. There are also twelve "Minor Prophets", so-called because the books attributed to them are shorter: Osee, Joel, Amos, Abdias, Jonah, Micheas, Nahum, Habakuk, Sophonias, Aggeus, Zachariah, and Malachi.

prudence. One of the four cardinal moral virtues (***vertu***), prudence is an intellectual habit that enables us to see what is virtuous and what is not and how to achieve the former and avoid the latter. In general it is a power of wisdom, intelligence, and foresight that resides in the intellect rather than the will and guides us with regard to the performance of other virtues. It is a moral preparedness to fashion means to a virtuous end.

pryvetee. Privacy in a secular sense, with variant spellings, but see the special application under ***Goddes pryvetee***.

purgatorie. Purgatory is the state of temporary rather than eternal punishment for sin: for venial sins, those not serious enough to incur damnation, and for the completion of "satisfaction" for mortal sins forgiven but not completely expiated on earth. It is traditionally a place of fire, though for example, not in Dante, where the soul is purged of its last remaining imperfections. The pains of purgatory, unlike those of ***hell***, do not include the pain of loss, because the souls in purgatory are guaranteed eventual passage into heaven; which, according to Aquinas and most others, the suffering souls know. In the second century Tertullian (***Tertulan***) asserted that the souls in purgatory could benefit from the prayers of the living. The merits and prayers of Jesus and the saints form a common fund or treasury for alleviating the chastisements of purgatory. Thus, the doctrine of purgatory is long-held and based on the Scriptural admonition that "It is a holy and wholesome thought to pray for the dead that they might be loosed from their sins" (2 Maccabees 12: 45). The Church cited multiple indications in Scripture of this future state (Matt. 5:25ff; Luke 12:58ff; John 5:16; 1 Cor. 3:15; Rev. 5:3,13). Arranging for a Mass to be said on behalf of the deceased was popular practice in Chaucer's time. Since the request for a Mass was usually accompanied by a monetary offering for the priest, the practice was subject to abuse and criticism, although an offering freely given could be an expression of genuine piety. Moreover, the living could gain indulgences, more frequently called pardons (***pardoun***), in the fourteenth century, on behalf of souls in purgatory. The Pardoner's Tale exemplifies some common practices, and abuses, concerning indulgences in Chaucer's day. (See ***dampnacioun***, ***peyne***, ***seint***, ***salvacioun***.)

PURVEAUNCE, PURVEIANCE, PURVEIAUNCE, PURVEYAUNCE, PURVEYINGE. Broadly, a kind of foresight, foreknowledge, or prudential wisdom. Its specific application is to Divine Providence (God's governance of the universe). There are four interconnected categories relevant to this governance: (1) God's powers (***foreknowynge***, ***Goddes privitee***); (2) human freedom (***fredom***); (3) fortune or chance; and (4) fate (***aventure***, ***fate***). Properly integrating these four factors in a coherent and theologically orthodox worldview is one of the most discussed problems in Medieval thought.

1. It would seem that divine perfection requires omniscience. Thus God must know everything, including the future. Furthermore, divine perfection also seems to require omnipotence: not only does God foresee all that will happen, but he also has the power to prevent undesirable future events. Must he also be so benevolent that he unfailingly wills to intervene to prevent future evil? Although it seems logically possible that an omniscient and omnipotent deity might not choose to intervene--and later Deists would hold such a belief—Medieval Christian faith (***faith***) is most fundamentally a belief in God's willing intervention and a trust in His benevolent Providence.
2. Belief in ***predestination*** is a further refinement of belief in Divine Providence. The doctrine of predestination, however, that God foreordains specific human events, up to and including the salvation or damnation of individuals, appears to contradict the attribution of free will to human agents. Free will is required for moral praise or blame, and so is necessary if human beings are to be held responsible for their own sins. And thus arose the main problem which caused controversy about Providence in the Middle Ages: if God has so designed the world, what place is there for free will?

   Moreover, if God has a plan for the good, why does he allow sin? One answer is that God does not cause, or even will, sin but wills both the freedom of the sinner and the good outcome that He will eventually draw out of their sins. This resolution may seem only to defer to some future time the inevitable conflict between God's sovereign Providence and human freedom to sin. That is, if God is always remediating human evil, are humans really free to be evil after all? The doctrine of hell (eternal punishment for unrepentant sinners) implies that human choices do indeed have ultimate and irreversible consequences; some humans may well suffer forever unredeemed. How could a good God allow that possibility? The more orthodox answer is that the workings of God are finally inscrutable and the compatibility of Providence and free will must be accepted as a mystery, part of the knowledge reserved to God (***Goddes privitee***), beyond human understanding.
3. One result of this theological agnosticism about the operations of Providence was the popular tendency to attribute to fortune (chance or accident rather than fate or design or the operation of free will) what is really part of a divine plan. So the theological doctrine of Providence did not keep the goddess Fortuna, the classical personification of ***fortune***, from being a prominent figure and force in Medieval literature.

This pagan goddess Fortuna was commonly invoked as an allegorical figure for the force of unpredictability. The fickleness of fortune was invoked as a reason for *contemptus mundi*, a distrust of the things of this world most notably demonstrated in the monastic life. The "wheel of fortune", on which human beings are sometimes up and sometimes down, was often cited as a reason to distrust wealth and happiness as transient. Even so, the more orthodox explanation of this ephemerality argued that what seems from a human point of view to be fortune is simply, *sub specie aeternitatis*, the inevitable working out of God's providential plan.

Even without these thorny problems about providence and predestination (foreordination), however, divine foreknowledge, especially God's foreknowledge of what human beings will do, posed a problem in itself: the knowledge that God has, if we are not to place limits on Him, of future events, also conflicted in the eyes of some with the doctrine of free will. Boethius (***Boece***) adverts to the problem, but the Medieval solution is in Aquinas and other scholastics who argued that God does not force all human choices, but rather simply knows what they will be. As early as St. Augustine, such theologians reasoned that mere (fore)knowledge on God's part is thus compatible with human freedom, the human faculty of choice. Since God exists in eternity, *i.e.*, outside of time, God's knowledge is not bound by time. All is present for Him at once; nothing is past or future. From a time-bound human perspective, however, God's eternal knowledge appears to be foreknowledge when it refers to what humans regard as the future. Necessarily, God timelessly knows what anyone will choose in time, but it is not the case that whatever is chosen, is chosen necessarily. That is, the necessity lies in the knowing, not in the choosing. Free will can be diminished, according to Aquinas, by a pattern of choices of lesser goods, but it can never entirely be removed. That is, repeated choices can become so habitual that one's future freedom to choose otherwise is impaired. In any case, the human will is not entirely free, although by definition it is always voluntary: Aquinas holds that we necessarily (and yet voluntarily) will our own happiness as our ultimate end, but we are free to choose among various means to that happiness, rightly or wrongly. Thus necessity and freedom are compatible in human volition.

4. If the human will can be both necessitated and free, might the divine will also be necessitated? Closely linked with the notion of divine necessity is the notion of ***fate***, the inescapable predetermination of future events by a force or forces beyond our control (for instance, astrologers typically believed that celestial bodies exercised such force on human affairs). The belief that fate is absolute posed a problem for Christian

thinkers, for if God is subject to fate, then His power and freedom are limited in a way that seems incompatible with his divinity. If, on the other hand, God is the master of fate, he can both foreknow and foreordain our futures; but to that extent, as we saw, there seems to be no room for us to choose freely and thus be praiseworthy or blameworthy. A limited fate, subject to God's control, however, is compatible with both God's divinity and human freedom. For instance, the sun may be fated to burn itself out and Jesus may be fated to return to earth at the end of time. (See also ***astrologye, fortune***.)

FURTHER READING: Reginald Garrigou-Lagrange, O.P., *Providence*, tr. Dom Bede Rose (St. Louis, MO & London: B. Herder Book Co., 1937); Mark John Farrelly, *Predestination, Grace and Free Will* (Westminster, MD: Newman Press, 1964); Thomas Forsyth Torrance, *Divine and Contingent Order* (New York: Oxford University Press, 1981); *Predestination and Free Will: Four Views of Divine Sovereignty and Human Freedom*, ed. David Basinger and Randall Basinger (Downer's Grove, IL: InterVarsity Press, 1986).

Rachel. Rachel was the wife of ***Jacob***, the daughter of ***Laban***, and the mother of ***Joseph***. Jacob labored for seven years to win Rachel but Laban gave him Leah. He then worked another seven years, increasingly put upon by Laban, after which Jacob and Rachel fled and were united (though Jacob also retained Leah as his wife.) The beauty of Rachel was legendary and is the source of the admirable tenacity of which Jacob is a model (Gen. 29-35).

Rapael. The role of the archangel Raphael is played out in the apocryphal Book of Tobias. He is one of the three archangels named in ***Scripture***. In the Book of Tobias, Raphael guides and instructs Tobias, throughout his eventful and finally successful journey, in determination, perspicacity, and how to have sex with the proper motives. For a summary of the story see ***Thobie***.

Rebekka, Rebekke. The wife of ***Isaac*** (Gen. 27). Rebecca devised the ruse by which her son ***Jacob*** was able to dispossess his elder brother Esau; he received Isaac's blessing while impersonating his hairy brother by wearing a goatskin in the presence of the aged, weak-eyed Isaac. Although it seems like rank trickery, Rebecca is cited as an example of good counsel, presumably because of the flourishing of the descendants of Jacob—the twelve tribes of Israel.

redempcioun. The restoration of mankind from the bondage of sin, incurred by the Fall of ***Adam***, through the merits of the suffering and death of *Christ*. Literally, redemption is a "buying back", the payment of a ransom. Because Adam's sin was an offense against the infinite God, only the infinite merits of Christ's Passion and Crucifixion, validated by the Resurrection, could provide condign ransom or satisfaction. Christ's redemption of mankind is the central fact of Christianity, the event which makes possible human ***salvation***.

(chanouns) regulers. Secular priests, as opposed to ordained monks or friars, who lived in communities, usually at a college, according to a rule similar to the monastic but not as stringent with regard to restriction to a ***cloister***.

religioun, relygioun. A body of doctrine or system of worship most notably applied in Chaucer to Christianity. The word occasionally referred more specifically to a community who lived according to a religious rule. The courtly love tradition adopted the notion of religion as a formal code of worship and applied it to the conventions of secular love in that highly artificial literary mode.

religious(e). Used as both an adjective and a noun for people who have committed themselves to a religious life, usually in community and according to a ***rule***, such as ***monks***, friars (***frere***), and nuns (***nonne***), though it could refer broadly to ecclesiastics in general as opposed to the laity.

There are two types of clergy distinguished by their ecclesiastical commitments: religious (or regular) and secular. Religious (in the narrow sense) are so called because they bind themselves (Latin, *religare*) by the three vows of poverty, chastity and obedience, and to the particular discipline (***rule***) of a religious order (such as the Benedictines, Dominicans, or Franciscans). Religious are also called "regulars" because they follow a *regula* (Latin for "rule"), especially if they have taken solemn vows. Religious who live in the confines of a monastery are called monks; mendicants, however, are called friars. In many religious orders, a new member first makes "simple" vows for a period of some years before making "solemn" vows; the distinction pertains to the seriousness of the commitment and the relative difficulty of being dispensed (excused) from these vows. Solemn vows are more binding than simple vows.

relike(e), relyk(e). Part of the body of a saint or an object associated with a saint or Christ or some event of religious significance. "Relicts" are things left behind. These were objects worthy of honor and veneration, used in seeking the intercession of the saints or the working of a miracle or to receive some less ambitious religious or secular benefits. In 2 Kings 13:21 a corpse which touches the prophet Elisha's bones is brought to life. Relics were not magical; they depended upon the intervention of God for their efficacy. Augustine (***Augustyn***), Jerome (**Jeremie**), Chrysostom (***John***), Gregory of Nazianzus, and virtually all the ***doctors*** of the Church recommended the veneration of relics, which sometimes had indulgences (***pardoun***) attached. There were many abuses by the unscrupulous including fraudulent relics, unseemly competition between religious groups over relics, and a bit of ghostly bone-picking. Doubts periodically arose about the authenticity of certain relics as their numbers and their use by unscrupulous preachers, like Chaucer's Pardoner, increased.

remedie, remedye. The relief of some problem or burden whether medical, legal, personal, or spiritual. As a religious term it refers to a means of counteracting sin or the disposition to sin and is often described, almost in an Aristotelian way, in terms of the relevant opposing virtue which could combat the sin in question.

repenta(u)nce. Contrition, *penitence*, sorrow for sins. (See ***sacrement.***)

reule, rule, rewle. A general moral rule or a norm for moral conduct; thus any religious law, custom, control, or even jurisdiction. However, its most concrete application is to a set of regulations governing a religious order of ***monks***, friars (***frere***), ***canons***, or nuns (***nonne***). The word is derived from the Latin *regula*, rule, and serves to distinguish regular clergy from secular or diocesan clergy—they live according to an articulated rule. The most famous and pervasive rule in the Middle Ages was the rule of St. Benedict, which was actually written by St. Benedict (***Benedight***) and stressed work and prayer. Other rules, such as the rule of St. Augustine (***Augustyn***), developed over time out of the writings of St. Augustine, were also influential. Friars, such as Dominicans and Franciscans, and nuns, like the Poor Clares, also lived according to a rule

The rule prescribed vows of poverty, chastity, and obedience, including obedience to the religious superior of the foundation, plus a way of life such as work, stability, and the cloistered life for monks; preaching and radical poverty for friars; ***cloister***, service and corporal works of mercy for nuns.

rightwisnesse, rightwysnesse. The cardinal moral virtue of ***justice*** whereby one rendered to others what is their due, neither more nor less. But the word can also suggest righteousness, moral integrity, or rectitude of life in general.

rode, rood(e). Any cross but especially the cross on which Christ was crucified. The rood was venerated because of its close association with the act of ***Redemption***. Early on it became a conventional symbol of Christianity, though the addition of Christ's body to the cross to make a true crucifix did not become popular until early in the Middle Ages. The True Cross was supposedly uncovered by St. Helena is Jerusalem in 318, whereupon relics, authentic and spurious, proliferated, especially because legend had it that pieces could be removed without diminishing the size of the True Cross. Although lost for a time in the tribulations of the Church of the Holy Sepulchre, a relic (***relike***) of the Cross is now believed to be present there; certainly enough purported relics appeared during the Middle Ages to supply a cemetery.

Ronyan, Ronyon. Although there are twelve Irish St. Ronans, the most notable was the seventh century St. Ronan of Iona referred to by Bede. A scholar and austere monk, St. Ronan supported the Roman custom for the placement of the celebration of Easter as opposed to an Irish tradition that had grown up. That he was supported by St. Finan, the Bishop of Lindisfarne, the other major scholarly monastic establishment of the period, added weight to his argument.

Sacked Freres. The Friars of the Patience of Jesus Christ, called the Friars of the Sack because of the roughness and simplicity of the cloth they wore as a symbol of extreme poverty, were a short-lived example of the flourishing and prestige of the mendicant orders in the thirteenth century.

Perhaps an offshoot of the Franciscans, they were founded in Provence, adopted the ***rule*** of St. Augustine (***Augustyn***), and were confirmed by Pope Alexander IV in 1255.

They expanded rapidly from 1256 to 1274 and established communities in London, Oxford, Lincoln, Bristol, Cambridge, and many European cities. Learned, rather like Dominicans, they concentrated their preaching in major cities. However, the envy of the secular clergy and the rivalry of Dominicans and Franciscans with all smaller orders encouraged the Council of Lyons (1274) to forbid the establishment of new mendicant orders and encouraged existing ones to merge with the Dominicans, Franciscans, Carmelites, or Augustinians. The conciliar decree did not endure, since the Jesuits were founded in 1540 as a mendicant order, but it did subvert the Sacked Friars.

SACREMENT, SACRAMENTZ. Sacraments are outward signs of inward grace, rituals which bring about the invisible reality which they signify visibly and publicly. Sometimes the word implied the specific sacrament of the Eucharist, or the Mass (***messe***) as a whole, or sometimes even God's mysteries in a very general sense.

In their sacramental view of creation, Chaucer's contemporaries read the Book of Nature and the Book of ***Scripture*** in much the same way: things were sign-vehicles for other things. In nature, God the Creator arranged visible creatures to signify invisible realities. In Scripture, God the supernatural author used the words of the human authors to signify things in nature with this deeper meaning. For instance, the rainbow signified God's covenant with Noah (Genesis 9:13), just as the flood signified moral purification. Accordingly, the waters of Baptism (***Baptesme***) bring about the inward purification that they signify and join the baptized person to the covenant community, the Church.

A sacrament, then, is an outward, visible sign of invisible ***grace***, instituted by Christ, celebrated by the Church until the end of time, and made efficacious by the power of the Holy Spirit. To say that the sacraments are "efficacious" is to say that the external rituals really accomplish inwardly what they signify outwardly, provided the individual recipient of the sacrament puts no obstacle in the way. Baptism, for example, is a washing with water that effects an interior cleansing from sin and a rebirth to the life of grace. The Eucharist or Mass is a sacrificial meal that effects atonement and union with Christ.

Thus there are three elements in each sacrament:

1. the action of the Spirit operating through the Church's prayer and worship.

2. the outward, visible sign special to each sacrament.
3. the action of Jesus at a particular place and time in history.

"There are three that testify: the Spirit and the water and the blood, and these three agree" (I John 5:7). As the sacrament of the Eucharist unites these three levels of reality, so does Baptism. (The "blood" refers to Jesus' death on the cross, the source of all the sacraments and the grace that flows from them. The "water" is the water of Baptism, the outward and material sign of an invisible reality and grace, namely, the washing away of sin and the birth of eternal life.)

In addition to Baptism and Eucharist, there are five other sacraments: Confirmation, Penance, Holy Orders, Matrimony, and Anointing of the Sick (also called "Extreme Unction" when it is celebrated in danger of death). In each case, we may distinguish the visible sign, the invisible grace or effect, the ordinary minister, and the eligible recipient.

For instance Confirmation, whose visible sign is the imposition of the hand of the minister (in England, usually a bishop) on the recipient and anointing with chrism (scented, blessed olive oil), effects the completion or spiritual maturity of the Christian who, by receiving Baptism and, if necessary, Penance, is eligible for this sacrament (see Acts 8:14-17 and 19:6). Baptism, Confirmation, and Eucharist together constitute the Sacraments of Initiation whereby someone enters into full membership in the Church. Penance and Anointing of the Sick are sacraments of healing, primarily in a spiritual sense but sometimes in a physical sense as well. Holy Orders and Matrimony are sacraments of service whereby Christians are equipped with the special graces needed for fulfilling their particular vocations to serve the Church and the world.

FURTHER READING: Karl Rahner, *The Church and the Sacraments* (New York: Herder and Herder, 1963); Colman E. O'Neill, O.P., *Sacramental Realism: A General Theory of the Sacraments* (Wilmington, DE: M. Glazier, 1983); Kenan B. Osborne, *Sacramental Theology: An Introduction* (New York: Paulist Press, 1988); Michael G. Lawler, *Symbol and Sacrament* (Omaha, NE: Creighton University Press, 1995).

Salamon, Salomon. The Biblical judge and king of Israel from about 974 to 937 B.C.E. (1 Kings 1-12; 2 Chron. 1-10). Solomon presided over a quiet period and devoted himself to the administration of justice, internal organization, and the erection of a national temple. Jehovah appeared to him in a dream and offered him a gift; Solomon chose wisdom. The bulk of the so-called "wisdom literature" was formerly attributed to him. In any case, he was renowned for justice, order, and sagacity. On the downside, he was given to public display manifested in the ambitions building program of his reign. And he is as renowned for the number of his wives and concubines as for the depth of his wisdom.

salvacio(u)n, savacio(u)n, savacyoun. Salvation is the achievement or condition of everlasting glory and life with God enjoying the Beatific Vision—the immediate perception of God. It is finally a gift of God's grace, even though it is achieved in a life of good works and charity. Salvation is the final goal of all Christians that gives meaning to human existence. The opposite of salvation is damnation: eternal separation from God. Just as man's ultimate happiness consists in eternal life with God, his ultimate misery (***hell***) is eternal separation from God. Those who die in the state of grace are saved; those who die in mortal (serious or grave) sin are damned. Since only what is holy can enter God's presence, those who die in the state of grace but hampered by the temporal effects of sin (*e.g.*, spiritual sluggishness or inordinate attachments to creatures) are purified of these effects through a transient condition called ***purgatorie***.

Medieval preaching often focused on the "Four Last Things": death, judgment, heaven and hell. God wills the salvation of all; man damns himself by sin; Christ opens the gates of heaven once again; man, united to Christ by acts of faith, works of love, and celebration of the sacraments, makes his *pilgrimage* to heaven via purgation either here or hereafter.

Samaritan (woman). Jesus was sitting by a well in the Samaritan town of Sychar when a woman came by for water. Jesus asked her for a drink but she resisted because Jews and Samaritans did not drink from the same vessels. He spoke to her of "the living water" that he would bring, and she asked for this water. Then Jesus asked her to bring her husband, and she said she has none. Jesus told her she was right because she has had five, thus the man she was living with was not truly her husband. She thereupon acknowledged Jesus as a prophet and he identified himself as the Messiah (John 4:4-30). Some Medieval theologians took this story as an object lesson against multiple ***marriages***; more saw it as an example of Christ extending his mission beyond the Jews.

Sampso(u)n. The exploits of Samson were numerous and impressive (Judges 14-16). He was promised to the barren wife of Manue as a son who would deliver Israel from the Philistines, though his hair must never be cut. Among other marvels, he killed a lion with his bare hands, burned the fields of the Philistines, and killed 1,000 of them with the jawbone of an ass.

The climax of his career was his liaison with Delilah (***Dalida***), who was charged to learn from him, by whatever duplicity necessary, the secret of his strength. When he revealed that it was in his hair, she cut it off and Samson was blinded and taken captive in humiliation to Gaza. However, when his hair grew back, he was brought out as a public display on the feast of Dagon, whereupon he pulled down the pillars of the temple and 3,000 Philistines perished with him. (See ***scripture***.)

Samuel. As a judge, Samuel was instrumental in defeating the Philistines. Although he reluctantly anointed Saul as king because the people wanted a king, eventually he rejected Saul. Finally, Samuel appeared, as a ghost, to Saul to reprove him for superstition in consulting the witch of Endor after Saul himself had forbidden consultations with spirits (1 Sam.-1 Kings 2:10).

Sarra. The wife of ***Abraham*** (Gen. 12-23). When Abraham went to Egypt, he pretended that Sara was his sister so they would not steal his wife. However, she was taken by the Pharaoh but restored to Abraham with a Divine admonition about his deceptive behavior.

Long barren, Sara gave permission to Abraham to have a child, Ishmael, by Hagar, but Sara became jealous of Hagar, and Ishmael was exiled. Finally, in her great age, Sara gave birth to ***Isaac***, thus prompting the prophet Isaiah to refer to her as the mother of the chosen people (Isaiah 51:2).

Sathan(as). The chief devil and supreme representative of evil. The name is often synonymous with Lucifer, through the latter name emphasizes the fiend's status as leader of the fallen ***angels***. The name Satan rather calls forth the tempter, who tempted Eve to eat of the fruit of the Tree of the Knowledge of Good and Evil (Gen. 3:1-7), who tempted Christ at the beginning of His public ministry (Luke 4:1-13), and who tempts every Christian.

satisfaccioun. Works of prayer, self-denial, and charity required of a penitent in expiation for sin as a requirement for ***absolution***. If satisfaction is not full on earth, then the soul must be cleansed in ***purgatory*** before entering heaven. Even if the guilt of sin is removed by absolution, satisfaction is required as a necessary condition for ***salvation***.

Scariot. See ***Judas***, the Apostle who betrayed Jesus.

sclaunder, sclaundre. Slander is a lie intended to discredit someone else. It may be a false accusation that impairs the reputation of another or something as pernicious as blasphemy (***blasphemynge***), which constitutes denigration and detraction of the Church. Its evil lies primarily in its malice, and satisfaction or reparation for this sin requires, as much as possible, the undoing of the evil done, usually by public knowledge

SCRIPTURE. The Bible, both the Hebrew Scripture (the Old Testament) and the Christian Scripture (the New Testament). Scripture refers to a collection of sacred writings composed over many centuries. They are "sacred" in several senses: (1) they refer to the *mirabilia Dei* (the wonderful things God does in human history); (2) they are held to be written under divine inspiration; and (3) they aim to make their hearers (or readers) holy by drawing them into a personal covenant with God, Who reproduces in the lives of believers what is narrated in Scripture. Diverse in genre, they are "writings" crystallized and selected, by synagogue or church, out of a wealth of oral tradition that both precedes them and continues even after the writings have taken definitive form. Thus taken together, they form "canons" or paradigms of orthodoxy. (The word "canon" also refers to the list of these books.)

In Chaucer's time the prevailing canon of Scripture was the Latin Vulgate (a popular or "vulgar" version for those whose vernacular was Latin), translated by St. Jerome (***Jeremie***) around 400 B.C.E. from Hebrew, Aramaic, and Greek originals. These Hebrew and Greek writings constituted earlier canons in their own right. Indeed, even when the Vulgate is regarded as the *editio typica* (standard edition) or *textus receptus* (accepted text), not it but the Hebrew and Greek originals are held to be divinely inspired.

The Hebrew Bible comprises the Torah, the Nevi'im, and the Kethuvim. The Torah ("Law" or "instruction" in Hebrew) comprises the five books traditionally ascribed to Moses: Genesis, Exodus, Leviticus, Numbers, and Deuteronomy. The Nevi'im ("prophets") are subdivided into the Earlier (Joshua, Judges, two books of Samuel, and two books of Kings) and Later (Isaiah, Jeremiah, and Ezechiel, plus the Twelve Minor Prophets—Hosea,

Joel, Amos, Obadiah, Jonah, Micah, Nahum, Habakkuk, Zephaniah, Haggai, Zechariah, and Malachi). The Kethuvim ("writings") are Psalms, Proverbs, Job, the Song of Songs, Ruth, Lamentations, Ecclesiastes, Esther, Daniel, Ezra, Nehemiah, and two books of Chronicles. When the Minor Prophets are taken together as a single book, and the two-volume works (Samuel, Kings, Chronicles, and Ezra-Nehemiah) are each counted as one, the thirty-nine books are counted as twenty-four. Sometimes the number is further reduced by similar combinations to twenty-two, the number of letters in the Hebrew alphabet. Since antiquity, and especially in the Middle Ages, some interpreters have paid painstaking attention to such numerological matters, seeing a hidden code in the arrangement of the writings—even down to the placement of individual characters in a line or page. Sometimes the arrangement is deliberate: for instance, some Christian compilers have placed the prophets last (rather than between Torah and Kethuvim) to emphasize a forward-looking link to the New Testament (see below); conversely, some Jewish compilers have avoided Malachi's prophecy of doom as the last word.

Beginning in the third century B.C.E., Greek-speaking Jews in Alexandria translated the Hebrew Bible into Greek. This Greek Bible, called the "Septuagint" (from the Latin word for seventy, the supposed number of translators), also included some writings for which we have no Hebrew original; these include Judith, Tobit, Wisdom of Solomon, Wisdom of Sirach (also called Ecclesiasticus), Baruch, several books of Maccabees, and additions to Esther and Daniel.

Taken up by Hellenistic Christians, the Greek Bible later included twenty-seven writings collectively known as the New Testament. These are principally of two kinds, evangelical and apostolic. The evangelical writings (the Synoptic Gospels of Matthew, Mark, and Luke; the Gospel of John) are "gospels" ("good spiels", a literal translation of *evangelia*) proclaiming the passion, death, and resurrection of Jesus as their central event. (The first three are called "Synoptic" because they are closely parallel and, seen together, "synoptically", are remarkable in both their convergences and divergences. This feature strongly suggests common source material combined with sufficient time for divergent traditions to develop in a widely scattered but united church.) As passion-resurrection narratives developed from earlier preaching, they acquired additional material: first, narratives of the public ministry of Jesus leading up to his arrest, and later, in two cases (Matthew and Luke), infancy narratives concerning Jesus' birth of the Virgin Mary. In Luke the journey from Galilee to Jerusalem structures the central narrative; this journey theme is also discernible in the other gospels, if not so clearly. Luke adds a sequel to his gospel, the Acts of the Apostles: a journey from Jerusalem to

Rome—two of the prime destinations for pious journeys (***pilgrimage***) in Chaucer's time. Along with these narratives is a wealth of proverbs, parables, and aphorisms attributed to the teaching of Jesus. In this respect, the development of the gospels is comparable to the *Canterbury Tales*: a skeletal journey is fleshed out with a potpourri of stories of various genres, often oral or folkish in idiom.

The second type, apostolic writings, are for the most part letters of apostles (missionaries commissioned by Jesus) to various churches. Some writers see a parallel to the Hebrew Bible's three-fold division into Law, Writings, and Prophets: in the case of the New Testament, the Gospels plus the Acts of the Apostles would correspond to the historical books highlighting the Law; the letters (epistles) would correspond to the didactic Writings; and the Book of Revelation (Apocalypse), to the Prophets.

Jerome's Latin Vulgate incorporated all three canons, Hebrew, Septuagint, and New Testament. In this context, then, the first two are called the Old Testament. Jerome himself distinguished between Old Testament books from the Hebrew Bible and those from only the Septuagint, placing the latter after the former as a sort of appendix. In subsequent editions of the Vulgate, however, the distinction was not always noted. The distinction between Old Testament and New Testament is always quite clear, however. The Latin word *testamentum* translates the Hebrew *berith* (Greek *diatheke*), meaning "covenant". Thus Scripture is regarded as a progressive series of covenants (sacred mutual commitments) between God and the first couple (Adam and Eve), then a household (Noah's), then a tribe (Abraham's), then a confederation of twelve tribes under Moses, then a national dynasty (David's), and finally (in Jesus) the whole human race, all linked by an unbroken ancestry.

When the phrase *novum testamentum* ("new testament" or "new covenant") occurs in the gospels, it is always connected with the blood of Jesus, which He identifies with the cup of wine that He offers his disciples at the Last Supper (the Passover meal on the evening of his death). In this way, multiple levels of meaning are superimposed. By the fourteenth century, a well-developed literary theory identified these levels as four: first the literal and then the three-fold spiritual (allegorical, moral or tropological, and anagogical) senses. This distinction is based on Paul's epistles. In 2 Corinthians 3:6 he writes that the "letter" (the literal) kills but the "spirit" (the spiritual) gives life; in Galatians 4:24, he uses the word "allegory" (*allegoreo* in Greek, a verb) to refer to a spiritual reading of a literal text of the Old Testament. "Tropological" comes from *trepein*, the Greek word for turning, in the sense of personal conversion; "anagogical" from the Greek word for leading upward, *i.e.*, to heaven as the final and eternal goal. Examples of this multi-level reading are scattered throughout

Scripture. Thus Scripture explicitly teaches how to read Scripture. As this teaching was developed in the Middle Ages, the literal level was not despised but seen as a foundation and rule on which the spiritual levels must be built. Aquinas (1225-1274) writes, "That signification whereby things signified by words have themselves also a signification is called the spiritual sense, which is based on the literal, and presupposes it ... Thus in Holy Scripture no confusion results, for all the senses are founded on one—the literal—from which alone can any argument be drawn, and not from those intended in allegory, as Augustine says. Nevertheless, nothing of Holy Scripture perishes on account of this, since nothing necessary to faith is contained under the spiritual sense which is not elsewhere put forward by the Scripture in its literal sense." (ST I.1.10)

On the literal level, for example, God's covenant with the Israelites under Moses was sealed with the blood of a sacrificed lamb. This blood, smeared on the doorposts at Passover, protected inhabitants from the destroying angel "passing over" Egypt. The first-born males of those not so protected perished. Allegorically, this event was regarded as a type (figure) of Jesus' bloody death on the cross. Tropologically, a Christian is saved from sin and death (both physical and spiritual) by a personal participation in Jesus' death through faith and love. This participation is both signified and effected by the celebration of the sacraments, especially the Eucharist, in which the bloody sacrifice on the cross is re-presented by the unbloody sacrifice of the Mass. Anagogically, he thereby partakes in the Lamb's Supper in the kingdom of heaven—here on earth sacramentally; in the age to come, completely (Revelation 19:7-10). (Note also Augustine [***Augustyn***] and his *Literal Commentary on Genesis*, which actually was a four-fold reading, well known in the fourteenth century. Dante's letter to Can Grande della Scala explicitly indicates that the *Comedy* is to be read on the four levels.)

So powerful was fourfold allegory as a heuristic device in the fourteenth century that some Medievalists (like D.W. Robertson, *A Preface to Chaucer*) have seen it as applicable throughout the religious and secular literature of the later Middle Ages. Although that view may be extreme, both the Clerk and the Nun's Priest invite us to read their Tales allegorically. Indeed, the Nun's Priest explicitly refers to the "significance" of all writing and the presence of a kernel of truth:

> For Seint Paul seith that al that writen is,
> To oure doctrine it is ywrite, ywis;
> Taketh the fruyt, and lat the chaf be stille. (VII, 3441-43)

Allegory aside, the preachers in the *Canterbury Tales* frequently refer to Scriptural authority, and the Wife of Bath revels in turning Scriptural citations to her own purposes.

Even the illiterate masses in Chaucer's time would be familiar with Scripture both from listening to preachers and from life-long exposure to visual representations of scenes from Scripture in church windows, sculptures, mosaics, frescoes, and so on. Wyclif and his followers, who translated Jerome's Vulgate into English, still insisted on the four levels.

FURTHER READING: Beryl Smalley, *The Study of the Bible in the Middle Ages* (Oxford: Clarendon Press, 3rd ed., 1983); D.W. Robertson, Jr., *A Preface To Chaucer: Studies in Medieval Perspectives* (Princeton: Princeton Univ. Press, 1962); Bertrand de Margerie, *An Introduction to the History of Exegesis*, 3 vol. (Petersham, MA: St. Bede's Publications, 1991); Manlio Simonetti, *Biblical Interpretation in the Early Church: An Historical Introduction to Patristic Exegesis*, tr. John A. Hughes, ed. Anders Bergquist and Markus Bockmuehl (Edinburgh: T&T Clark, 1994); Thomas F. Torrance, *Divine Meaning: Studies in Patristic Hermeneutics* (Edinburgh: T&T Clark, 1995).

secte. Although a sect may be a philosophical school of thought, the word is more often reserved for an identifiable set of religious beliefs and practices, usually non-Christian or heretical. (See ***heresye***.)

seint(e), seynt(e). Anyone who has achieved salvation is a saint, but the designation is ordinarily reserved for persons of heroic virtue who have undergone the formal process of canonization by the Church and are therefore sanctioned as worthy of veneration and capable of intercession. The awareness of saints, even when only attested by their frequent appearance in mild oaths, was characteristic of the fourteenth century. Saints were in fact taken very seriously as a part of spiritual life because of their intercessory power with God, and the lives of the saints were looked to for guidance and inspiration. The *Legenda Aurea*, the definitive Medieval collection of saints' lives, was compiled by by Jacobus de Voraigne (1231-1298) in about 1265, and was frequently drawn upon by fourteenth century preachers for instruction and examples (*exempla*.)

In addition, the Church as a spiritual network (the "Communion of Saints") is helped by the prayers and merits of each member but hurt by the sins of each member, no matter how secret. This is obvious in the case of social acts: a single act of kindness can have repercussions into the far distant future, as the beneficiary of that act may become a little more kind to someone else, who in turn benefits a third person, and so on. So, too, with hurtful acts. This solidarity in good and evil is less obvious with interior acts (thoughts, prayers, attitudes) but no less real, given the spiritual interconnectedness of all the faithful, both living and dead.

Seint-Jame. The shrine of Santiago, St. James Compostela in Spain. It was one of the major ***pilgrimage*** destinations in the Middle Ages.

semycope. A short outer cloak commonly worn by ***monks*** and friars (***frere***); it did not have any special liturgical use as a vestment.

sermo(u)n(e). A publicly spoken religious discourse, though the homilies of many ***Doctors*** and learned clerics were recorded and preserved for their moral and didactic values. The sermon became a highly stylized form of discourse in the Middle Ages, admired to the point of being considered entertaining as well as salutary. Usually based on a religious text, the sermon proceeded to interpret the text and offer examples and applications for the lives of the auditors.

Sermons could be delivered in a public place but were characteristically presented in a Church. Other than the ***parson*** or ***canon*** in his own Church, formal approval by the episcopal authority was required of preachers, many of the best of whom were friars (***frere***) like the Dominicans. Given the necessity to suit the doctrine to the understanding of the common people, sermons were one of the main conduits for religious instruction for a people to whom the written ***Scriptures*** were not easily accessible. Sermons became a regular part of the Mass (***messe***), delivered between the readings of the Lessons from the Epistles and Gospels and the Offertory.

service, servise, servyce, servyse. A religious rite or liturgy. The most common application was to the Mass (***messe***) but the could be applied to any communal religious observation such as Benediction or public recitation of the canonical offices such as Lauds or Vespers.

sexteyn. A sacristan, someone who is in charge of protecting and preserving the physical structure of the church or cathedral as well as its contents such as altars, relics, books, vestments, and objects or vessels used in the liturgy. In the fourteenth century, the sexton was usually a cleric in minor orders, and thus permitted to marry. In a monastery, however, one of the ***monks*** would perform these functions. His duties extended to a variety of ancillary functions, including the keeping of the keys (for the security of the edifice), the ringing of bells to summon the congregation or to note special occasions, and the digging of graves.

shapen. The verb that is used to denote God's creation of the universe and sometimes applied to the supposed operations of fate. (See ***fate***, ***foreknowynge***.)

shrift(e), shryfte. ***Confession*** or the ***sacrament*** of ***Penance***, requiring contrition (sorrow), auricular confession, a purpose of amendment, and an intent of ***satisfaction*** by prayers, self-denial, acts of charity, and alms giving, in order to receive ***absolution***.

Simon Magus. Simon Magus, associated by his name with magical arts, was converted by the preaching of Philip the Deacon. When Peter and John came to Samaria, Simon offered them money to receive the power which they had of bestowing the Spirit by the laying on of hands. He was chastised by Peter (Acts 8:9-24). Certainly a sorcerer, and the source of the word "simony" for the buying of religious power, favor, or position, Simon was characterized in second century legends as a heretic, an opponent of Christian doctrine, and a false Messiah.

Simon the Pharisee. Simon complained when a prostitute, sometimes identified as ***Mary Magdalen***, approached Jesus, wept for her sins, and bathed Jesus's feet with her tears (Luke 7:36-50). Jesus told Simon the parable of the two men in debt, one for fifty and the other for 500 pieces of silver, and asked who would be more grateful for cancellation of his debt. The narrative concludes with Jesus' praise for Mary's humility and repentance.

sin, sinne, syn, synne. Generally, an offence against God. Original sin is the Fall of Adam and Eve, the guilt of which is imputed to all, and release from which becomes possible through Baptism only after the Redemption by Christ. More often, however, sin refers to "actual" sin, offenses against God committed after Baptism: the breaking of any of the Ten

Commandments or any properly enacted laws of the Church. At its base, sin is a deviation from the good of God's creation, the choice of a lesser good over a greater good, and, therefore a deviation from right reason. It is a violation of the proper love of God, self, or neighbor.

"Actual sin" may be mortal or venial. Mortal, or serious, sin is death to the soul and requires serious matter, full consideration, and total acquiescence of the will. Venial, or less serious, sin lacks one or more of these three conditions and does not in itself result in damnation.

slouthe, slewthe. Indolence or laziness, one of the seven deadly sins (***deedly synnes***). Sloth is the moral weakness, inattention, indolence, or lack of steadfast purpose that interferes with the living of the Christian life. It enervates the Christian life and obviates acts of charity (***charite***).

somnour, somonour An officer of the ecclesiastical court. Not necessarily a cleric, a summoner was charged, ordinarily by the archdeacon (***ercedeken***), to summon defendants to the ecclesiastical court (***Court Cristien***) to answer for matters over which that court had jurisdiction, such as failure to pay tithes, adultery, bigamy, or matters of inheritance. The ecclesiastical courts also had jurisdiction over any offense committed by a member of the clergy. Consequently, summoners wielded an ominous kind of power which, in the fourteenth century, they sometimes abused.

Less often, the word might refer to a comparable officer of the secular court or of a guild, but Chaucer's kind is the ecclesiastical. The face of the ecclesiastical, or church, courts most commonly seen by the general public in England in the Middle Ages was that of the summoner, or "apparitor", whose primary function was to "summon" and convey the accused for trial, judgment, and sentencing. If the two summoners who appear in the *Canterbury Tales* are at all representative, then the integrity of the office and, by extension, of the ecclesiastical courts had become highly suspect by the later fourteenth century. The summoner in the "Friar's Tale" and the pilgrim summoner, who is devastatingly described in the General Prologue and who tells a retaliatory tale about friars, are corrupt, even menacing, representatives of their institution.

soul(e), sowle. The soul is the spirit that inheres in human beings. It is the seat of rationality and will, which differentiate human beings from the beasts. As spirit, the soul is indestructible. As a moral entity, it is destined for eternal ***salvation*** or ***damnation***, though after the Second Coming of

Christ it will, regardless of its fate, be re-united with the body. Thus it is the salvation of the soul, because of its immortality and its ultimate recognition of God as its greatest good and purpose for being, that is the primary goal of every Christian.

subdekne. The lowest of the sacred, or major, clerical orders. The subdeacon's role was to prepare the sacramental wine, pour the water into the wine, present the chalice and paten, read the Epistle prescribed for the day, and generally assist the deacon (***dekne***) at Mass. Eventually, the office devolved simply into a step on the way to the priesthood.

surquidrie. That aspect of ***pride***, one of the seven deadly sins (***deedly synnes***), that has particularly to do with presuming upon one's own powers or upon the mercy of God for *salvation*. The more common Medieval form of this word is surquidie and the second "r" may be a scribal error.

Susanne, Susanna. Suzannah was the beautiful young bride of Joachim (Daniel 13). Two elders lustfully watched her as she relaxed nude in what she believed to be the privacy of her garden. The elders departed but, driven by lust, returned separately, awkwardly met each other, and agreed to hide in the garden and either force themselves on her sexually or publicly accuse her of adultery with a young man. She refused them and was sentenced to death. A young man, Daniel, objected to the conviction and cross-examined the two elders separately. They contradicted each other on the location of the adultery (one says under a clove tree, one under a yew), and they are themselves sentenced to death for bringing the false accusation. The story is admonitory concerning bearing false witness and the responsibility of people in positions of authority.

Symoun, Seint. The suggestion of some that this is Simon Magus is improbable, since he, though a convert, was reproved by St. Peter (Acts 8:9-24) for trying to buy the power of infusing the Spirit; he is the source of the word "simony," and in any case he was never canonized. A bit more possible is the apostle known as Simon the Zealot for the intensity of his religious fervor as a Jew even before he was called by Christ. More probable still is St. Simon (Simion) Stylites, one of the early Eastern hermits, who undertook total fasts on pillars beginning at nine feet in height and ultimately graduating to fifty feet.

The most attractive candidate, however, is St. Simon Stock (1165-1265), born in Kent and therefore also called St. Simon Anglus. He was the sixth general of the Carmelite order and founded Carmelite houses in major university towns: Cambridge (1248), Oxford and Paris (1260), and Bologna (1260).

Synay. Mt. Sinai, where Moses received the Ten Commandments (Exodus 19:17-20). It is sometimes identified with Mt. Horeb, though the latter may actually refer to the whole mountainous region surrounding Mt. Sinai. It was the refuge of many anchorites during the persecutions in the third century.

Te Deum. A hymn of praise: *Te Deum Laudamus* (We praise You, God.) Something similar appears in the ***rule*** for ***monks*** of St. Caesarius (502 C.E.). The hymn was sung at specified times in the divine office, especially Matins. It was also sung on special occasions such as the election of a Pope, the consecration of a Bishop, the ***profession*** of a religious, or on the occasion of some spectacular or apparently miraculous event.

Templers. The Knights Templar were the first of the "military orders" of monks. In 1118, Hugues de Payens and eight companions took a perpetual vow, in the presence of the patriarch (***patriarke***) of Jerusalem, to defend the Christian Holy Land. The order was confirmed at the Council of Troyes (1128), at which *St. Bernard* of Clairvaux played a significant role, and they adopted the rule of St. Benedict as modified by the Cistercians, assuming the white habit but adding a red cross.

In addition to the three vows of poverty, chastity, and obedience, they vowed to protect the Holy Land from the Muslim Saracens. The order was comprised of four ranks: knights (heavy cavalry), sergeants (light cavalry), farmers (administrators of the temporal affairs of the order), and chaplains (clerical ministers.) From the first, they were an anomaly in mission and position: monks devoted to warfare and with special privileges. For example, they were responsible directly to the Pope, paid no Church taxes, and were immune from interdict. As early as 1156, clergy in the Holy Land tried to restrict some of their privileges, especially the economic ones. When one considers that they also received economic tribute from most of the sovereigns of Europe and that they plundered what they conquered, it is not surprising that their treasury grew rapidly, developing such great wealth and power that they became the unofficial bankers of Europe.

There were never large numbers present in the Holy Land, no more than 400 knights at one time. But they were furious and unrelenting soldiers, killing over 20,000 "pagans" in less than 200 years. Their own mortality rate was so high, however, that, in desperation, they accepted even excommunicates and waived the ordinary rules for entry into monastic life.

The older ***Hospitallers*** at first welcomed them, then reviled them, but without the controversy and distrust characteristic of other enemies, who distrusted the Templars because of their temporal success and a mysterious secret rite of initiation. In 1307, Philip the Fair, for his own political reasons, ordered the arrest of all the Templars in France. Increasingly, their secrecy brought charges of idolatry, sodomy, and parodies of the Mass and sacraments. They were dissolved by Papal decree in 1311 and their members were urged to join the Hospitallers or other orders.

Tertulan. Tertullian, born about 160 at Carthage, converted to Christianity from paganism in mid-life. In *Ad Nationes* and *Apologeticus*, he attacks heretics and persecutors of Christians and defends Christian orthodoxy and the apostolic tradition. His theology was austere if not severe, forbidding second marriages and arguing that some sins, such as idolatry, blasphemy, adultery, and pride, were unforgivable. He was ascetic and acerbic and that is probably what led him to join the Montanist heretics early in the third century and later found his own sect. The Montanists were a strange schismatic and heretical group in the Near East, who had ecstatic visions and professed a radical asceticism to the point of seeking out martyrdom.

theme. The biblical text on which a ***sermon*** was based.

(ad) Thimotheum. St. Paul's Epistle to Timothy. This epistle contains a notable warning against covetousness (***covetise***), and a strong admonition against errors, especially those contained in fables.

Thobie. The Book of Tobias, in the Vulgate but not part of the Hebrew canon, is one of the most charming books of the Bible. Tobit, a devout and faithful man, is blinded by bird droppings as he lies in his garden. His wife reproaches him and wishes for death as their economic circumstances decline. Meanwhile, a certain Sara has seven husbands killed by a demon before consummation of the marriages. God solves both problems.

Tobit's son Tobias is sent to collect a debt from a distant source, and the archangel Raphael appears as his constant guide and advisor during this journey. Tobias catches a large fish, and Raphael instructs him to keep the heart, the liver, and the gall. They retrieve the money owed and set out for home. They come upon Sara, and Tobias falls in love. On the advice of Raphael, Tobias burns the liver and heart of the fish, which casts out the demon and enables Tobias to consummate a "marriage" with Sara (though the consummation does precede the marriage.) Tobias, Sara, and Raphael return to Tobit. After the wedding of Tobias and Sara, they offer half of the recovered debt to Raphael. He refuses but tells Tobias to hold the gall of the fish in one hand and blow on the eyes of Tobit, whose sight is thereby restored. Raphael identifies himself as one of the seven archangels that stand before the throne of God, they celebrate, and Tobias lives a long, happy life.

One reference in Chaucer seems to be to Tobit ("Tale of Melibee") and one to Tobias ("Parson's Tale").

Thomas of Inde, Ynde. According to legend the Apostle St. Thomas, the doubter who would not accept Christ's Resurrection until he touched His wounds, traveled East to convert India. The story is found in ***St. Ambrose***, St. Jerome (***Jeremie***), and St. Gregory of Tours, all based apparently on the doubtful *Acta Thomae* of the early third century.

Thomas (of Kent), Seint. St. Thomas a Becket (1118-1170) studied canon law at Bologna and Auxerre. Archdeacon (***ercedeken***) of ***Canterbury***, he was ordained in 1154. The young Henry II made Thomas Lord Chancellor at the age of thirty-six (Henry himself was only twenty-four), giving Thomas great temporal power. In 1162 he was consecrated Archbishop of Canterbury, but continued his austere life that included ***fasting***, wearing a hairshirt, and keeping protracted vigils. More devout than secular, he came into conflict with his friend Henry by asserting Church and clerical privileges, notably the right of "criminous clerks" to trial by the ecclesiastical courts (or at least not double jeopardy by subsequent trial in civil courts.) Consequently, he resisted the Constitutions of Clarendon, which restricted the authority of the ecclesiastical courts (***Court Cristien***). Harassed by Henry, Thomas took refuge with the Cistercians at Pontiguy. After bitter negotiations, in which Thomas threatened Henry with excommunication and Henry threatened retaliation against the Cistercians,

Thomas returned to Canterbury where four knights accosted him, returned with armed men, and murdered him in the Cathedral.

Popular reaction on behalf of Thomas was astonishing. Extraordinary devotion to the "martyred" archbishop sprang up almost immediately. Henry was forced to do public penance and was scourged at Becket's tomb. Thomas a Becket was canonized in 1173, and for the rest of the Middle Ages, Canterbury was one of the wealthiest and most famous shrines in Europe and the prime pilgrimage of destination in England.

Thymothee. 1. Timotheus was a Syrian general in 2 Maccabees 8-9. Over 20,000 of his men were killed in his second encounter with ***Judas Machabeus***. In 2 Maccabees 10, Timotheus was defeated again and killed. 2. Timothy, the recipient of Paul's ***Epistle***, was a trusted disciple of ***Paul***, frequently mentioned in other Pauline Epistles, and called "the angel of the Church of Ephesus". In Paul's Epistle to Timothy, he counsels against covetousness and warns Timothy about errors, especially those that arise from belief in fables (fictional narratives that seem to have a moral point).

tithes. Tithing, the reservation of one-tenth of one's income for the Church, is mentioned in the Hebrew Scriptures. In the Middle Ages, payment of tithes to the Church or a clerical institution was required. Although at first spontaneous in the early Church, the first indications of obligation appear in a letter from bishops assembled in Tours (567) and in the canons of the Council of Macon (585). Claiming that tithes were a matter of divine law, the Church made them obligatory in all Christendom. English law recognized tithes before the Norman Conquest, and they became part of written law in the Statute of Winchester (1285). At first payable to the bishop, later they were collected by the parish priest and enforced by the ecclesiastical courts (***Court Cristien***).

trinitee. The doctrine of the Trinity, one of the central mysteries of the Church, holds that there are three persons in one God, *i.e.*, one Divine nature: from the Father, associated with mercy and power, proceeds the Son (***Christ***), associated with wisdom, and from the eternal love of Father and Son proceeds the Holy Ghost, associated with love and grace. The Son is "begotten" of the Father by means of an eternal generation and the Holy Ghost is generated by an eternal procession from Father and Son; therefore the three persons are co-equal and coeval.

The doctrine was frequently contested, especially by fourth-century Arians, who denied the divinity of Christ, but it was affirmed early by Theophilus of Antioch (180) and Tertullian (***Tertulan***). The orthodox doctrine was incorporated into the Nicene and Apostles' Creeds and basic liturgies. St. Augustine's *De Trinitate* is the foundational orthodox philosophical treatment of the Trinity.

The doctrine of the Trinity is closely linked with the doctrines of the Incarnation and the ***Redemption***: were Jesus not wholly a divine person, he could not offer sufficient satisfaction for man's offense against the majesty of God since an infinite majesty is offended infinitely ("lese majeste"); were he not distinct from God the Father, there would be no one who could accept the satisfaction that he offered. Yet were he not completely human as well, God-become-man, it would not be man who offered satisfaction, and man would remain unredeemed.

Tubal. ***Lamech's*** son Jubal (Gen. 4:19-22). Jubal is called "the father of all such as handle the harp or organ". Jubal, Lamech's son by Adah, was frequently confused with Lamech's son by Zillah, Tubalcain, the patron of blacksmiths and metal workers.

Urban, Seint. Of the eight Urbans who were Pope, Urban I (r. 222-230) was the only one to be canonized. Nothing is known of his life except from the "Acts of St. Cecilia", a fifth-century work of doubtful authority but many copies. In it Urban is credited with baptizing Cecilia's husband and brother-in-law and with effecting multitudinous conversions.

Valentyn(e), Seint. According to the *Acts of the Martyrs*, records of martyrs made by notaries of the Court, February 14 was connected with two St. Valentines in the third century, a priest at Rome and the Bishop of Interamna, as well as with an obscure individual who suffered and died in Africa. None of the three is historically associated with love or courtship. There was, however, a tradition in England and France that associated "St. Valentine" with the day on which birds gathered to pair. It became the occasion for the exchange of love letters and tokens, and St. Valentine thereby may have become associated with love. The first written record of the association is in Chaucer's *Parliament of Fowls*, but it appears later in Gower, Lydgate, and the Paston Letters.

venial(e), venyal. A less serious sin than a mortal, or deadly, sin. It must be sorrowed for and ***satisfaction*** must be performed, but there is no absolute need for ***confession*** and it is not a bar to salvation. Nevertheless, venial sins must be purged by penitential acts in this life and/or suffering in ***purgatory***.

vertu(e). As virtue has a general secular sense of power, force, or strength, it has a general religious meaning of good moral behavior. More specifically, it is defined as a habit. Augustine says "Virtue is a good habit consistent with our nature." Aquinas says it is "an operative habit, essentially good". That is to say, it is a habit associated with a faculty of the soul that disposes it towards good moral acts. Thus, morality is more a matter of who we are than of what we do. What we do, though, largely shapes who we are (and vice versa). Seven virtues were stressed throughout the Middle Ages: the four classical or cardinal virtues of prudence, justice, fortitude, and temperance, and the three theological virtues of faith, hope, and charity. The former list was a commonplace as early as the fourth century B.C.E. and is discussed by Plato and Aristotle. Hence, these are "classical" virtues. They are "cardinal" ("hinge") virtues because all the other moral virtues in some way hang from them (just as the cardinal sins are sources of all other sins). They can be acquired by natural human effort, as well as infused supernaturally by God. In contrast, the theological virtues are entirely supernatural in the sense that unaided human nature cannot acquire them; rather, they must be infused by the grace of God. Charity is the form of all the virtues and necessary for gaining any supernatural merit.

vicaire, vicarie, viker, vicary. In the secular world a vicar is a representative or deputy, one who substitutes for the main official. In the fourteenth-century Church, a vicar was a cleric acting as priest in a parish in place of the ***parson***. The vicar was capable of performing all of the priestly functions. The term was also used for the representative of a religious community designated to act on its behalf especially in the collection of ***tithes*** due the community.

vigilies. Services held the evening before a feast day or guild festival. Wives of local dignitaries and elected officials would have pride of place in the processions which were part of the ceremony. The vigil (day before) of a religious feast has technical ecclesiastical significance, but Chaucer does not use the term in this sense.

virgine. A virgin was anyone who abstained perpetually from sex. Usually the word is associated with the virtue or religious commitment required of clergy and members of all religious ***orders***. *The* Virgin is the Blessed Virgin Mary (***Marie, Seinte***), the mother of Jesus.

virginitee. The state of abstinence from sex, virginity was a devout religious practice. Secular clergy (clergy belonging to a particular geographic unit [a diocese] instead of a religious order) do not take the three vows of ***poverty***, ***chastity***, and ***obedience***, although in Chaucer's time they were expected to be both celibate and chaste. "Celibate" properly means "unmarried"; chastity is a type of temperance whereby one's sexual activity is in keeping with one's state of life. Thus, chastity for a married couple channels sexuality so as to foster an indissoluble and exclusive love of the man and woman for each other, as well as optimal conditions for bearing and rearing children. Chaucer's Parson reflects this two-fold purpose of marital sexuality in pointing out the venial sinfulness of a husband "whan he useth his wyf, withouten sovereyn desir of engendrure to the honour of God, or for the entente to yelde to his wyf the dette of his body" (PsT, X, 374). On the other hand, chastity for a celibate entails an unconsummated sexuality which looks forward either to earthly marriage or to heavenly union of the soul with her bridegroom, Christ.

Although all clergy and members of religious orders were committed to virginity, the state is most commonly associated with the radical sexual purity of women. From the early Church virginity was seen as a higher commitment than marriage, perhaps in imitation of Christ's implied virginity. It is asserted by many Fathers and Doctors of the Church, notably St. Jerome (***Jeremie***), who ascetically and acerbically insists on female virginity for reasons of religious devotion and self-control. St. Jerome preferred male virginity as well, but saw women as especially dangerous if not virginal. The anti-feminists thrived on St. Jerome's views.

vowe. A solemn promise made to God to perform an action or undertake a course of life that will be pleasing to Him. The most specific application is to the vows of poverty, chastity, and obedience required of ***religious***, but Chaucer never seems to use the term in this sense.

wanhope. See ***despeir***.

White Monkes. Cistercians were called White Monks because of their white habit. The Cistercians, in an attempt to reform the Benedictine order, insisted upon more stringent adherence to St. Benedict's (***Benedight***) ***rule***, established in Citeaux in 1098. The most powerful proponent of Cistercian reforms was ***St. Bernard*** of Clairvaux, who entered the order in 1112. The Cistercians flourished in the twelfth century, but began to decline in the middle of the fourteenth century, probably because the great dispersion of monasteries that their success had brought led to creeping laxity, a lack of uniformity in adherence to the reformed rule, and disputes among superiors about details in the charter.

wimpel, wympel, wymple, wympul. A piece of white linen cloth worn by women, folded so as to cover the top of the head, the sides of the face, the chin, and the throat. It became part of the habit of nuns by the fourteenth century, usually arranged in ripples or layers and intended as a badge of modesty.

Ysaac, Ysaak. The son of ***Abraham*** and the second of the early patriarchs of Judaism (Gen. 15-35). For long he and his wife Rebecca (***Rebekka***) had no children. Then they had twins, Esau and ***Jacob***. Isaac favored Esau, but was tricked by Jacob in a ruse devised by Rebecca. Jacob deceived Isaac, who was old and had failing eyesight, when he posed as Esau by covering himself with a goatskin (Esau was hairier), and received Isaac's blessing intended for Esau. Jacob thereby became the father of the twelve tribes and thus the father of the Israelites.

Ysaye, Isaye. Biblical prophet, author of the Book of Isaiah. He described the religious degeneration of Judah in the latter eighth century B.C. Having received a heavenly call to decry the corruption of the society and its deviations from the Mosaic Law, he presented vivid oracles and warnings, in a powerful style, of the punishment of evil and reward of good that would come. One of the four major prophets, he is cited as the foremost by the author of the Book of Ecclesiasticus.

Ysidre, Seint. St. Isidore of Seville (c. 570-636) was a prolific writer and proponent of learning. At the Fourth Council of Toledo he convinced all bishops that there should be seminaries in their cathedral cities. He appreciated Aristotle and the Greek philosophers generally. He made the first attempt at a Summa, a compendium of knowledge of a sort characteristic of the Middle Ages. His *Etymologiae* was used as a textbook throughout the Middle Ages. Bishop of Seville and revered scholar, he is considered by some the last of the great Latin Fathers of the Church.

Yve, Seint. Possibly St. Ives or Yves of Brittany (1253-1303), the patron of lawyers. More likely St. Ives of Chartres (c. 1040-1116), the Bishop of Chartres who was imprisoned for opposing Philip I's desire to divorce his wife and marry Bertrade of Anjou. Mostly known for his letters and sermons, this St. Ives was much interested in resolving contradictions that appeared in the works of the Church Fathers. He exerted an intellectual influence on Hugh of St. Victor, Abelard, and Gratian.

Zakarie, Zacharie. The Biblical prophet Zechariah was one of the twelve minor prophets. He criticized pride and moral corruption in eight visions. For a list of the minor prophets, see ***prophete***.

Appendix

Annunciation: **Marie, Seinte**

Ascension: **Crist**

Assumption: **Marie, Seinte**

Beatitudes: **conseil**

Blessed Virgin Mary: **Marie, Seinte**

Capital sins: **deedly synnes**

Cardinal virtues: **vertu(e); prudence; justice; fortitudo**

Clergy: **pre(e)st, bisshop; canon; clerk**

College, collegiate: **cano(u)n**

Crucifixion: **Crist**

Ecclesiastical Court: **Court Cristien**

Excommunication: **Court Cristien; ercedekenes curs**

Gratian: (Book of) **Decrees**

Incarnation: **C(h)rist**

Indulgences: **pardoun**

Legenda Aurea: **seint(e)**

Liturgical hours: **monk**

Liturgy: **messe; monk**

Mendicancy: **frer(e)**

Monasticism: **monk; nonne; Benedight; rule; Augustyns**

New Testament: **Scripture**

Paganism: **hethenesse, payen**

Pilgrims: **palmeres**

Predestination: **purveaunce; fate**

Providence: **purveaunce**

Resurrection: **C(h)rist**

Theological virtues: **vertu; faith; hope; charite(e)**

Bibliography

Adam, K., *The Christ of Faith: The Christology of the Church*, tr. Joyce Crick, New York: New American Library, 1962.

Adams, M.M., *What Sort of Human Nature: Medieval Philosophy and the Systematics of Christology*, Milwaukee: Marquette University Press, 1999.

Amiot, F., *History of The Mass*, New York: Hawthorn Books Publishers, 1959.

Aston, M., *Lollards And Reformers: Images And Literacy in Late Medieval Religion*, London: Hambledon Press, 1984.

Basinger, D. and Basinger, R. (eds.), *Predestination and Free Will: Four Views of Divine Sovereignty and Human Freedom*, Downer's Grove, IL: InterVarsity Press, 1986.

Bokenkotter, T.S., *A Concise History Of The Catholic Church*, Garden City, N.Y.: Doubleday, 1977.

Brown, P.R.L., *The Cult Of The Saints: Its Rise And Function in Latin Christianity*, Chicago: University of Chicago Press, 1981.

Cabie, R., *History of the Mass*, tr. L. J. Johnson Portland, OR: Oregon Catholic Press, 1992.

Catholic Encyclopedia, New York: Robert Appleton Company, 1907.

Chadwick, O., *A History of Christianity*, New York: St. Martin's Press, 1996.

Crichton, J.D., *Christian Celebration: The Mass*, London: G. Chapman, 1971.

Cross, F.L., and Livingstone, E.A. (eds.), *The Oxford Dictionary Of The Christian Church*, New York: Oxford University Press, 1997. 3rd edn.

Cunneen, S., *In Search of Mary: The Woman and the Symbol*, New York: Ballantine Books, 1996.

Daniélou, J., *The Bible and the Liturgy*, Notre Dame, IN: University of Notre Dame Press, 1956.

Daniel-Rops, H., *This is the Mass*, New York: Hawthorn Books, 1958, 1965.

Eliade, M., Adams, C.J., et al. (eds.) *Encyclopedia of Religion*, New York: Macmillan, 1987.

Farrelly, M.J., *Predestination, Grace and Free Will*, Westminster, MD: Newman Press, 1964.

Finucane, R.C., *Miracles And Pilgrims: Popular Beliefs In Medieval England*, Totowa, N.J.: Rowman and Littlefield, 1977.

Gambero, L., *Mary and the Fathers of the Church*, tr. T. Buffer, San Francisco: Ignatius Press, c. 1999.

Garrigou-Lagrange, R., O.P., *Providence*, tr. Dom Bede Rose, St. Louis, MO & London: B. Herder Book Co., 1937.

Garrigou-Lagrange, R., O.P., *Predestination*, tr. Dom Bede Rose, St. Louis, MO & London: B. Herder Book Co., 1939.

Grady, T. (ed.), *Signatures of Grace: Catholic Writers on the Sacraments*, NY: Dutton, 2000.

Grillmeier, A., *Christ in Christian Tradition*, tr. J. Bowden, Atlanta: John Knox Press, 1975. 2nd rev. edn.

Hall, C.A., *Reading Scripture With the Church Fathers*, Downer's Grove, IL: InterVarsity Press, 1998.

Halligan, N., O.P., *The Sacraments and Their Celebration*, New York, NY: Alba House, c. 1986.

Husslein, J., *The Mass of the Apostles The Eucharist: Its Nature, Earliest History and Present Application*, Kenedy and Sons, 1929.

Jelly, F.M., O.P., *Madonna: Mary in the Catholic Tradition*, Huntington, IN: Our Sunday Visitor, 1986.

Jungmann, J.A., *The Mass of the Roman Rite, Its Origins and Development Missarum Sollemnia.*, tr. F.A. Brunner, rev. C.K. Riepe, New York: Benziger Bros., 1959 new rev. and abridged edn.

Jungmann, J.A., *The Early Liturgy, to the Time of Gregory the Great*, tr. F.A. Brunner London: Darton, Longman & Todd, 1960 [c. 1959].

Kilmartin, E.J., *Christian Liturgy: Theology and Practice*, Kansas City: Sheed and Ward, 1988.

Klauser, T., *Kleine abendländische Liturgiegeschichte*, English: *A Short History of the Western Liturgy: An Account and Some Reflections*, tr. J. Halliburton, Oxford & New York: Oxford University Press, 1979 2nd edn.

Lawler, M.G., *Symbol and Sacrament*, Omaha, NE: Creighton University Press, 1995.

Marchos, J., *The Catholic Sacraments*, Wilmington, DE: M. Glazier, 1983.

Margerie, B., *An Introduction to the History of Exegesis* [Introduction a l'histoire de l'exegese, English], Petersham, MA: St. Bede's Publ., 1991.

McHugh, J., *The Mother of Jesus in the New Testament*, Garden City, N.Y.: Doubleday, 1975.

Midmer, R., *English Mediaeval Monasteries, 1066-1540: A Summary*, Athens: University of Georgia Press, 1979.

Miegge, G., *The Virgin Mary: The Roman* Catholic *Marian Doctrine*, tr. J.A. Mackay Philadelphia: Westminster Press, 1955.

Milman, H., *History of Latin Christianity*. London: J. Murray, 1883-1901.

Nichols, O.P., *The Holy Eucharist: from the New Testament to Pope John Paul II*, Dublin: Veritas, c. 1991.

O'Carroll, M., C.S.Sp., *Theotokos: A Theological Encyclopedia of the Blessed Virgin Mary*, Wilmington, DE: M. Glazier, c. 1982.

O'Collins, G., *Christology: A Biblical, Historical, and Systematic Study of Jesus*, New York: Oxford University Press, 1996.

O'Neill, C.E., O.P., *Meeting Christ in the Sacraments*, Staten Island, NY: Alba House, 1964.

O'Neill, C.E., O.P., *Sacramental Realism: A General Theory of the Sacraments*, Wilmington, DE: M. Glazier, 1983.

Osborne, K., *Sacramental Theology: An Introduction*, New York: Paulist Press, 1988.

Pallen, C.B. and Wynne, J.J. (eds.), *The New Catholic Dictionary*, New York: The Universal Knowledge Foundation, 1929.

Pelikan, J., *The Riddle Of Roman Catholicism*, New York: Abingdon Press, 1959.

Pelikan, J., *The Christian Tradition: A History Of The Development Of Doctrine*, Chicago: University of Chicago Press, 1971-1989.

Pelikan, J., *Mary Through the Centuries: Her Place in the History of Culture*, New Haven: Yale University Press, c. 1996.

Platt, C., *The Abbeys And Priories Of Medieval England*, NY: Fordham University Press, 1984.

Rahner, K., *The Church and the Sacraments*, New York: Herder and Herder, 1963.

Robertson, D.W., Jr., *A Preface To Chaucer: Studies In Medieval Perspectives*, Princeton: Princeton Univ. Press, 1962.

Simonetti, M., *Biblical Interpretation in the Early Church: An Historical Introduction to Patristic Exegesis* [Profilo storico dell'esegesi patristica, English], tr. J.A. Hughes; eds. A. Bergquist and M. Bockmuehl, Edinburgh: T&T Clark, 1994.

Smalley, B., *The Study of the Bible in the Middle Ages*, Oxford: Clarendon Press, 1941. 3rd rev. edn. c. 1983.

Steuart, B., *The Development of Christian Worship: An Outline of Liturgical History*, London: Longmans Green and Co., 1953.

Strayer, J.R. (ed.), *Dictionary of the Middle Ages*, New York: Scribner, 1982-1989.

Swanson, R.N., *Church And Society In Late Medieval England*, New York: Blackwell, 1989.

Thomas, T.F., *Divine and Contingent Order*, New York: Oxford University Press, 1981.

Thompson, W., *Christology and Spirituality*, New York: Crossroad, 1991.

Torrance, T.F., *Divine Meaning: Studies in Patristic Hermeneutics*, Edinburgh: T&T Clark, 1995.

Vassall-Phillips, O.R., *The Mother of Christ: or, The Blessed Virgin Mary in Catholic Tradition, Theology, and Devotion*, London: Burns, Oates and Washbourne, 1936.